THE LITTLE BOOK OF
TRUE GHOST STORIES

THE LITTLE BOOK OF
TRUE
GHOST
STORIES

Echo Bodine

Cover design by Jim Warner
Cover image copyright © Silent 47

Hampton Roads Publishing Company, Inc.
Charlottesville, VA 22906
www.hrpub.com

Library of Congress Cataloging-in-Publication Data is available on request.

ISBN: 978-1-57174-650-4

TCP

10 9 8 7 6 5 4 3 2 1
Printed on acid-free paper in Canada

To Roman

CONTENTS

Acknowledgments

I would like to thank JoAn Hall for putting all the work into the book that you did. You were a life saver.

Greg Brandenburgh for publishing the book and for always pushing me to make it better.

To my totally cool family, the Bodines.

To all the formerly stuck souls who taught me about ghosts.

To my brother, Michael, for always walking ahead of me on jobs and making this difficult work fun to do.

PREFACE

Many years ago I discovered one of the "benefits" I gained from developing my psychic abilities: I have the ability to see dead people—souls (spirits) living on the other side and souls (ghosts) still lingering on the earth plane.

The last forty years have been quite a journey. I discovered the world of ghosts; why they choose to remain earthbound; why some are afraid to go to heaven; what their day-to-day existence is like.

They're all such different characters: a hobo who didn't feel worthy of going to heaven. A group of mentally ill ghosts who remained on the property of the asylum they lived in, years after it had been torn down. Ghosts who prevent houses from selling because they like the family that's living there. Deceased teenage ghosts who roam the halls of high schools along with deceased teachers who miss their jobs.

I met a ghost who sings opera and a ghost named Sherrie who had been murdered and chose to stay here rather than face her killer who had committed suicide. I saw a ghost roaming the halls of St. Paul City Hall in her wedding dress, waiting for her boyfriend to arrive so they could get married.

I was once slapped on the back of the neck by a ghost who told me to get out of the warehouse he "worked in;" another ghost tried pushing me down the very stairs she had jumped to her death from over a hundred years before.

I've felt them walk through me, and I've seen them come right up to my face and try to take my breath away, hoping to gain power from my energy.

I've seen them in people's garages, attics, showers, bedrooms, basements, and kitchens. I've witnessed ghosts sitting in chairs, lying on beds, pretending to dine at dinner tables, staring out windows, riding elevators, sitting in classrooms, acting on stage, sitting in a television audience. I've seen ghosts in homes, churches, businesses, hospitals, school dorms, libraries, tanning parlors, farms, funeral homes, treatment centers, cabins, flower shops, and day care centers. Anywhere that people hang out, ghosts hang out too.

This book shares the world of ghosts as seen through the eyes of a real-life ghostbuster. Many of the stories also feature my psychic brother, Michael. (He has written a great book called *Growing Up Psychic* that you'll want to check out for more psychic adventures.)

Each story you read is as close to accurate as possible. Only the names have been changed.

INTRODUCTION

Before we dive into the world of ghosts, I'd like to start at the beginning and tell you how this all got started.

It was a typical evening at our home in the fall of 1965. I was seventeen years old. Sitting around the table after dinner were my parents, my two brothers, my sister, and me. My brother said he was going downstairs to practice on his new drum set. He was just beginning to learn how to play the drums, so, needless to say, his playing still sounded a little rough. The rest of us were carrying on with our different after-dinner conversations, trying to avoid the dishes for as long as possible, when, all of a sudden, we all stopped talking and turned our attention to music coming from the den. It was *really good,* not the usual beginner stuff we were used to hearing from my brother. We all looked at Dad, expecting he would somehow know why my brother was playing like a pro. My father suggested that we must be hearing the new Sandy Nelson record he had just bought my brother, and even though that answer didn't feel accurate, we continued to listen for signs of what was really going on downstairs.

About a minute later, my brother came flying up the stairs, totally freaked out. "Did you hear it, did you hear it?" he said, and we all answered, "Yes, what was it?" My brother explained that he was sitting at his drum set, practicing his normal fare, when out of nowhere, a white figure floated through the door and over to him. He said that he closed his eyes, hoping it would disappear, but even with his eyes closed, he could still see this whitish male figure standing in front of the drum set. This "guy" took my brother's hands and basically played through him, making the really beautiful music that we heard from the dining table. He tried letting go of the drumsticks, but was not able to release them from his hands until this "man" floated back across the room and through the door. My brother was so upset that he said he was never going down to the den again.

We were all pretty blown away. My mom, who usually kept a cool head, called a friend of hers who had been to a medium in England and was living in St. Paul. Fortunately, she was able to reach the psychic medium, Mrs. Eve Olson. Mrs. Olson told my mother that she'd been expecting the call. After my mother related the story of what had happened with my brother and the drumming, Mrs. Olson told her that the spirit was my brother's guardian angel, Dr. Fitzgerald. When this doctor was living on earth he was also a drummer, and because he was my brother's angel, he was going to work with him and teach him many things. She also told Mom that she and each of her four children had some very unique gifts and that she wanted to see Mom and her oldest daughter (me) for a reading. We were all speechless.

What did all of this mean? Did we all have guardian angels? Why could my brother see his, when the rest of us couldn't? What did "unique gifts" mean? My siblings and I inundated our parents with questions that they had no clue how to answer. I was so frightened by the thought that my own guardian angel might appear to me that night that I began sleeping with the lights on.

Within a week my mom and I went to see Mrs. Olson.

On the drive from our south suburban home to her home in West St. Paul, Mom and I were full of anticipation. I wondered what this medium from England would be like. Did she read a crystal ball? Was her house filled with black cats? Did she wear big dangling earrings and tie long scarves around her head? I couldn't imagine what kind of unique gifts she was referring to and what she would tell me. At that point in my life, the only things I was interested in knowing were when I was going to meet Mr. Right and how many children I was going to have.

As we approached Mrs. Olson's front door, my stomach filled with butterflies. I was so nervous, and I just wanted to go away and pretend this wasn't happening.

Much to my surprise, a very sweet, petite, round woman with an English accent answered the door and invited us in. She was more like a grandma than any gypsy I had seen on TV (back then the only psychics we saw on TV were gypsies). There were no black cats or crystal balls. Mrs. Olson introduced us to her very normal-looking husband and told my mother to have a seat in the living room while she escorted me into her "reading room."

When I wondered aloud if everyone was this nervous on their first visit, Mrs. Olson reassured me that nothing frightening was going to happen. She explained to me that the glass of water on the table was for the spirits—it gave them energy. She also said that my spirit guides, who were supposedly helpers from the other side, were the source from which she was getting information about me.

I sat frozen in my chair, waiting for something to fly through the room or for the water in the glass to disappear. Instead, this very gentle medium from England told me that I was born with all four of the psychic abilities and with the gift of healing. Stunned, I listened as she told me that I came to earth this lifetime to be a well-known psychic and spiritual healer. I would write books, be on TV and radio, travel, and teach others how to develop their abilities. I would be known throughout the world.

I was a shy teenager and couldn't imagine myself doing any of that—let alone being famous. I planned to go to college to become a social worker, and had always imagined myself as a wife and mother someday. I told Mrs. Olson that I was going to college, that I didn't think I had any psychic abilities, and that I just wanted to have a normal life. She told me that I had been using my abilities my whole life and had grown accustomed to them. She said that once I understood what they were, I would recognize them. She also said that I did not come to earth this lifetime to have a normal life—that I came to be a teacher and healer.

Something inside of me knew that what she was saying was true, but I didn't want to know these things because it all seemed so scary and totally out of my reality. I didn't know how to think about it.

In my mother's reading, Mrs. Olson told her that she too had these gifts and that she would be a gifted psychic. So would my baby brother, Michael. She said that my sister, Nikki, would not develop her abilities until she was in her forties, and that all of us would someday use our gifts to help people. Everything she told Mom has since come true.

After that first session with Mrs. Olson, Mom and I became very curious about our abilities. We went to occult bookstores and started reading whatever was available. We bought an Ouija board, and our home slowly became a haven for mischievous, noisy spirits. They would bang on the walls and make sounds like footsteps or someone typing on a typewriter. Life became scary for all of us. We never knew what to expect. It was as if we had opened a door to something we didn't understand, but we couldn't get it closed again.

We had psychic experiences almost daily. My younger brother, Michael, could see and hear spirits and my sister, Nikki, who was oblivious to most of the supernatural goings-on in the house, saw a spirit even before I did. Lights blinked on and off. Radios and TVs turned on and off by themselves. Objects moved from room to room— the stuffed animals in my bedroom moved by themselves. We constantly felt like we were being watched.

Sometime during the first year of all of this, a psychic, spiritualist minister in Minneapolis called my mom and said that her spirit guides had told her to teach eight people in the Twin Cities how to develop their abilities. My name and my mom's name were on the list. She gave Mom her address and said she expected to see us for classes that started in a week.

My mom and I were so freaked out by everything going on already that we weren't sure how much more involved we wanted to get, but we decided to go the first night just to see what it was all about. We were pleasantly surprised to find that everyone in class seemed as normal as we were—they expressed the same uncertainties that we had. We ended up going to these classes on and off for close to two years.

I can't say that I took to psychic development like a duck takes to water. It took me a long time to develop my abilities fully because I let my intellect get in the way most of the time. I analyzed all the psychic information that came to me, and I questioned everything that my teacher said. I was looking for something concrete that I could hold onto. I wanted it to all make sense on a rational level. Letting go of my mainstream thinking and believing and accepting things that couldn't be seen by the human eye or proven by science was very scary for me. My skepticism made my psychic development a lot harder than it had to be, but I'm glad I was as skeptical as I was. I didn't accept everything hook, line, and sinker; I acquired my new beliefs slowly over time.

When I started doing ghosthunting jobs over forty years ago with my brother, Michael, I never would have guessed that they would become such an important part of my work. The first time I went on a ghost job, it was more out of curiosity than a desire to get involved with ghosts. I had no idea that ghosts were souls of deceased people. I grew up watching *Casper the Friendly Ghost* cartoons on Saturday mornings; I thought ghosts were just white energy blobs. I didn't think of them as actual people.

I remember when I finally put two and two together and realized that ghosts are really the souls of deceased people who haven't gone on to heaven. I became quite intrigued with the whole concept of why a soul would choose to not go on to the other side.

Each of the stories in this book is a true-life ghost story that I've experienced firsthand.

WHAT IS A GHOST?

It was a dark and stormy night. The thunder shook the trees from their very roots. Bolts of lightning struck the earth's surface, burning holes deep into the soil.

What was inside the house was ten times as frightening. The Livingstons had ghosts. Several black, monstrous, floating creatures were knocking lamps off tables, pushing pictures off walls, and tossing clothes out of closets and drawers. They killed the family dog, Fluffy, and ate the guinea pig, Hector. The cat spewed brown foam from its mouth and moaned incessantly. The Livingstons wanted to know when this reign of terror was going to stop.

Green smoke burned out of the nostrils of these unwelcome guests. Their red eyes glared in the dark. Purple slime dripped from their mouths. Nothing could stop or tame these horrible visitors from the world beyond. They were out to destroy the family home and drive Mr. and Mrs. Livingston insane. They hated with a vengeance. They showed no mercy for the children the day they tied them up and chopped off their toes. They were horrible, villainous monsters slowly taking over and destroying this beautiful nineteenth-century Victorian home.

Just as an evil-looking specter loomed toward Mr. Livingston wielding a bloody ax, someone in the back room hollered, "Cut, let's do that scene over!" And we realize it's Hollywood making another movie about ghosts!

A Ghost's Life

A ghost's life is probably not at all what you would think it would be. I want to give you a picture of what life is really like for a ghost.

Imagine a very large, dark, open space filled with hundreds of thousands of souls. They look like people, but many have blank stares on their faces and are so self-absorbed they aren't even aware that there are other beings floating around beside them. Many of them appear as if they're going somewhere, but in reality they're not. They're just milling around, stuck in time. There's no happiness in this place. No sense of life or purpose.

These are not highly evolved souls. They are immature in their soul's development and often suspicious that anyone who might come to "take them home" is simply the Devil in disguise.

Many souls are quite confused about life after death; others are aware of what's going on and know they could move on to heaven but choose to remain in the astral plane—a vast wasteland of nothingness—after their physical body dies. Some believe death is simply a vacuum of emptiness, and rather than reach out to others for help with their plight, they simply choose to stay stuck. Many prefer to hold on to their former lives and identities. Many are filled with self-pity, anger, resentments, fear, or self-loathing. They wander this place, stuck in time and avoiding change.

From where they are, every one of them can see a beautiful light glowing at the "front door" of the other side. They all see the road that leads to heaven and many times a day see souls making that journey into the light, but for their various reasons none of these souls want anything to do with that place. Some believe that if they even try to go there, God will snatch them up and send them straight to hell. Some don't believe they have a right to go to heaven; others don't believe in a heaven and think this special road might actually lead to hell. They refuse to go in case they're being tricked.

There are souls who have committed suicide and are afraid to take the road home for fear that they won't be allowed in or will be sent to hell for the "sin" of taking their own life. There are souls who were addicted to things of the physical body such as food, alcohol, drugs, and sex who aren't ready to let go of their addictions. They hang out in the astral plane, hoping to find a way to continue to get high or experience their addiction. The majority of souls simply want to hang on to who they were and not move on.

How Houses Become Haunted

I want you to imagine that this vast empty space is the next dimension just above the earth plane. These stuck souls can see our homes, businesses, schools, and all the living people on earth. Sometimes they get lonely, bored, or restless and decide to look around for some action. And that's when they become ghosts—when they come to earth and make themselves known to us through their antics. Even though most of them are loners and rarely socialize, many are drawn to houses that have other earthbound spirits in them because they like knowing there are others around them. This is how a home becomes haunted.

At some point the ghosts realize that they can manipulate energy. When they get bored or want to get a kick out of frightening people, some of them start playing tricks to get people's attention. If your lights, TV, or radio turn on and off, it's a safe bet that this is the work of one of these antsy earthbound spirits. They learn that fear and anger are two powerful emotions with a lot of energy, so they'll try to create these emotions by frightening people. Then they'll either breathe in this energy to boost their own or use it to make more scary things happen, which then generates more energy, and so on.

People living in haunted houses often know that something isn't right, but they don't know how to interpret what's happening or what to do about it. They might see something wispy or floating out of the corner of their eye, but they chalk it up to an overactive imagination or something they saw on television. They might feel afraid, but they don't take it seriously—and that gets the ghost feeling even more rambunctious. That's usually when ghosts will begin tapping on the walls or making footstep sounds or pulling clothes out of closets. Or moving things from room to room, jangling door knobs, turning wastebaskets upside down, tipping things over, or making mumbling sounds. They might walk through a person, giving him the feeling of a cold breeze whooshing through his body. Ghosts do all of this to get a rise out of people in hopes of sucking up their fear energy.

Earthbound spirits who were addicts in life will look around for the home of an addict with the same addiction so they can enter the addict and continue to experience their preferred high. This is one way a person becomes possessed.

These stories are real. This is what ghosts are really about. They are angry, stuck, miserable, rebellious, lonely, depressed, afraid of God, and/or formerly addicted souls. They are lost. Many don't want to accept that they've died, and most do not want to move on.

In their opinion, the next best thing to being alive is hanging out on earth, and they'll do almost anything to get our attention. I've rarely met a ghost who doesn't eventually get bored being all alone and want some kind of contact. They'll look for a home inhabited by other ghosts, but they'll also look for homes that have sensitive (psychic) people in them. They can tell this by looking at our auras (the energy around our bodies). The intensity of the colors tells them which members of the household will respond to them the best.

For example, an intellectual's aura tends to have a lot of yellow in it. Ghosts usually stay away from people with yellow auras because they learn early on that intellectuals are always looking for rational explanations for everything—the ghosts can't get a rise out of them.

On the other hand, people with pink in their auras are very sensitive and open to having psychic experiences. Ghosts who find teenagers with pink in their auras feel like they've hit the jackpot, because teenagers are almost always open to having "ghostly encounters" and are less likely to tell the spirits to get lost.

Before we go any further into the world of ghosts and spirits, I want to start with the basics.

The Difference Between Ghosts and Spirits

When we physically die, our souls come out of our bodies, and, most of the time, we move on to the other side. Once in a while a soul will choose, for one reason or another, not to go on to the other side. It will choose to stay here on earth, which is where the "earth" from the term "earthbound spirit" comes from.

Ghost Fact

The difference between a ghost and a spirit is very simple: both are souls who are no longer living in a body, but a ghost is a soul who has remained on earth, and a spirit is a soul who has moved on to the other side and begun a new life there. A spirit can come to this side to visit, but it will return home; spirits are not stuck here on earth. Ghosts are.

A soul is made up of energy. It looks like the physical body it inhabited except that it's transparent. Some parapsychologists call the soul the *body double* because it looks so much like the physical body when it was alive. I've also seen the soul appear as a streak of light or blob of energy. When a soul appears in body form, it will also appear to be wearing clothing similar to something the person wore when in the body. A friend of mine who was killed visited me a few times after his death, and he always appeared to have on the same blue jeans and camel-colored leather jacket that he frequently wore when he was alive. My teacher told us that souls do this so they won't frighten us, just in case we are able to see them.

I saw the comedian Sam Kinison about a week after he died, walking around on the other side and shaking people's hands. He appeared to be wearing the long coat, tennis shoes, and hat he always wore in his comedy routine. One of the misconceptions about life after death is that we all wear robes and angel wings once we die. If Sam Kinison, or anyone deceased for that matter, were walking around in flowing gowns and angel wings, we would never recognize anyone. . . . And then there's the issue of scaring us half to death if they appeared to us!

Also common, and a little eerie, is that ghosts will sometimes only appear from the waist up or as just a head! This is because their energy is low and that's all they are able to manifest. It doesn't mean they're not all there—it just means that's as visible as they can make themselves at the time. As time passes they will build up their energy and be able to appear in full form.

There are basically two kinds of spirits: souls who remain earthbound, which we call ghosts, and souls who move on to the other side or heaven, which are commonly referred to as spirits. Spirits will visit us on earth, but they will always go home again to the other side.

Ghosts and spirits will both appear just as they did in their last life, which can make it pretty confusing to tell who's who. The giveaway, usually, is that ghosts tend to have an unhappy look to them, whereas spirits seem almost to glow. A ghost will usually seem depressed or irritable, with a certain blankness to his face, like the lights are on but no one's home. His aura is usually grayish, and you get the sense that he's got unfinished business. Spirits, on the other hand, tend to look radiant. Within a couple of weeks of crossing over, they appear younger, with no signs of stress on their face. Being with them, you sense that they are looking forward to resting and healing from their recent life experience. They're happy to be reunited with loved ones and radiate a sense of anticipation about their new life.

THE GHOST WHO LIKED LIQUOR

It was wintertime, 1969. I was twenty-one years old and still living at home. We'd had a lot of spirit activity in our house since getting on this path, but until then I hadn't actually *seen* any spirits.

The first time I ever went to someone's house intentionally looking for a ghost, I had no idea what I was doing. I was pretty scared and still believed that ghosts were scary monsters who looked all whitish and weird—like they had no form and were just blobs of scary stuff!

What made this fun was that it was a friend of my mom's who suspected she had a ghost, so Mom and I went on the "job" together. The drive over to Carol's that night felt a lot like that drive over to Mrs. Olson's; we didn't know what to expect, and our imaginations were running wild. Carol had told us that there were strange sounds coming from the attic and she felt as if someone were watching her family. She said that her son was a recovering alcoholic and was having a terrible time staying sober. She wondered if there was some kind of negative influence in the house preventing her son from maintaining his sobriety. She also said they could hear a choir singing church music, which was interesting because their home had at one time been a church.

On the drive over, I was full of questions for my mom. What were we looking for? Did Carol really think she might have a ghost? What did a ghost look like? What were we going to do if we found one? I thought we should probably turn around and go home. Finding ghosts was not something I wanted to do.

When we pulled up to Carol's house, I imagined seeing scary things in all the windows. I was sure the ghosts were all watching me, ready to pounce on me as soon as I walked in the door. As usual, Mom was pretty calm, which always helped me feel more grounded. We kidded around with Carol for a while, trying to lighten things up. Looking back, we were probably just stalling; I don't think any of us really wanted to go to the attic and deal with whatever was there. The analytical part of me thought that it was probably just noisy pipes and there was nothing to make a fuss about.

Our chitchat ended, and it was time to see what was up in the attic. Slowly we made our way up the stairs. I'm sure I had one eye open and the other one closed as we reached the top of the staircase. I had myself scared silly.

At first glance everything seemed normal. The usual boxes and stored furniture were piled here and there. Then, slowly, images began coming into focus. At first all I saw was a very faint image of a family of four standing across the room from us. It was quite strange to look at this almost invisible family. They looked so strained and old, so frightened. My rational mind immediately tried to explain it all away. I told myself I was making it up, that ghosts weren't people. Ghosts didn't look like that. They were supposed to be scary-looking. These were simply transparent people who didn't look scary at all—just tired, old, and afraid.

They had a gray appearance to them. The man looked crabby and seemed angry that we were able to see him. The woman started talking to us as soon as she realized we could see her. I'm sure my mouth was hanging wide open as I watched this transparent female tell us about her death and explain that she was trapped in this house by her husband. She said he had been an alcoholic and a smoker. He had passed out one night after drinking and his cigarette burned their house down. All four family members perished in the fire. The woman said her husband would not let any of them go on to the other side because he was afraid of being punished by God for killing his family. I was flabbergasted.

I looked at mom and could tell by the shocked look on her face that she could hear this woman as well. I asked her what we should do, and we came up with the idea to just tell the ghosts that they couldn't stay at Carol's house anymore. They had to leave because they were frightening Carol's family. Mom got some psychic information through her clairvoyance (psychic sight in the third eye located in the forehead) and clairaudience (psychic hearing; her guides speaking to her). She learned that the male spirit had been entering Carol's son's body from time to time in order to taste alcohol and cigarettes, and that was why it was difficult for her son to maintain sobriety. After telling them that they needed to leave, Mom and I were anxious to leave, too. This was all so creepy. We had no idea what we were doing or how to get rid of the ghosts. They did disappear, giving us the illusion that they had left, but my guess is that they probably just stepped outside or went over to the neighbors' to make us think they were gone. We didn't hear a church choir or see any other spirits as we walked through the rest of the house. I think our fear shut us down psychically. There certainly was a feeling that there were more spirits there than we cared to know about, but I just wanted to go home. I wasn't ready to deal with ghosts yet!

Ghost Fact

The female ghost in this story could have taken her children and moved on to the other side anytime she wanted, but she allowed her husband to control her in death as she undoubtedly had in life. Every one of us has to discover our own power at some point in our soul's development and stop giving it away to others. It's part of setting ourselves free.

The Ghost Who Tried to Push Me Down the Stairs

The next time we went to psychic class, Mom and I told our teacher Birdie what had happened at Carol's. She told us that in the future we shouldn't show any fear because spirits can draw on fear energy and make themselves bigger. She said that if we're ever around spirits and feel afraid, we should say a prayer, such as the Lord's Prayer, to help us feel more in control. As she was saying all this, I told myself it didn't matter because I had no intention of going into a haunted house ever gain. Little did I know that shortly thereafter Birdie's advice would come in very handy.

One evening after my church youth group meeting, Dean, one of the guys in the group, told me he had heard through the grapevine that I had psychic abilities. He wanted to know if I would come over and check out his attic, because there were sounds of footsteps and strange noises that neither he nor his roommates could explain. He said that every day for the past few weeks when they came home from work, they would find one of their baby kittens dead, crushed by something heavy. All I could think about was Birdie's advice about not showing fear when dealing with a spirit. I wondered if I was strong enough to go see what was killing Dean's kittens, and I told him that even though I wasn't very experienced in this area, I would give it a try.

Our whole youth group excitedly piled into cars and took off for Dean's house. I wanted to help, but I also felt a lot of fear about what I was walking into. I asked my spirit guides to help me, but I wasn't too good at hearing them yet.

On the drive over I tried to explain to myself what the noises might be. Maybe it was noisy pipes, or perhaps Dean and his roommates had overactive imaginations. Maybe one of the roommates was playing some kind of trick on everyone. I was trying to find a logical explanation for why everything was happening so that I could feel less fearful about going in and investigating, but something inside me was telling me that there was a lot more going on in Dean's house than just noisy pipes.

When we got to Dean's house, I asked everyone to wait downstairs and told Dean to walk up to the attic with me. I knew that when I opened up psychically I would be able to feel everyone else's fears in addition to my own, so I decided the fewer people around, the better. As we were approaching the top of the very steep steps that led to the attic, I could psychically see an image of a male spirit dressed in black clothing, standing on the other side of the door. I felt so much fear that I didn't think I could go in there. The ghost appeared to have dark hair and almost black eyes. His face was contorted with anger. I told Dean we needed to go downstairs and get everyone to come up with us. I no longer cared about feeling everyone's fear; I needed reinforcements!

As we were turning around to go back down the stairs, I could see the male spirit coming at me very fast. He floated right through the closed door and literally put his two hands on my back and pushed very hard. I threw my arm out a broken window, which just happened to be to my right, and was able to catch myself from falling. My heart was pounding so hard that I thought it was going to come out of my chest. The total fear I had been feeling just moments before now changed to anger, and I was determined to do whatever I could to get this ghost out of there.

Dean and I went downstairs and explained what had just happened. Everyone, including the skeptics, was anxious to go upstairs and see if they could see or sense this negative entity. We all headed up the stairs, scared half out of our wits.

I told the group that it was important not to show any fear and that if we got scared we should say the Lord's Prayer for protection, but I don't know if anyone heard me. No one else in our group had developed psychic abilities or had ever seen a ghost, but everyone was up for whatever was going to happen.

When we got to the top of the stairs, everything was quiet. We opened up the attic door and nothing seemed unusual. There were several boxes piled high over to the right, and to the left there was a mattress on the floor with a little nightstand. Dean explained that someone actually lived up there, but apparently she had never seen or felt anything strange. He said she was kind of odd herself, and he thought maybe she just blended in with all the strange goings-on.

We decided to sit in a circle on the floor and hold hands. There was a light directly above our heads, which we turned off. We just sat there on the floor, waiting for something to happen. I began to see a very faint image of two forms standing over by the boxes. One was short, maybe only three-and-a-half-feet tall. I found myself staring at that one because I was curious about why it was so small. Then she came into view—a little girl about four years old. She was holding hands with the other form, which slowly took the shape of a woman.

They began to float toward us. Several members of our group reported later that they could see them as well. All of a sudden, the man dressed in black emerged from the left side of the room. The woman and little girl seemed really frightened and darted behind the boxes. Then the man-ghost lunged toward our group. I knew everyone else saw him too, because several people gasped at once.

I quickly reminded the group to say the Lord's Prayer and not to show fear, but it was evidently too late, because the man was getting bigger and bigger right before our eyes. He appeared about twelve feet tall and kept looming toward the group, obviously trying to scare us. I could see by the look on his face that he was thoroughly enjoying himself at our expense. Every time we said the prayer, he would shrink in size. Amazing. Birdie had been right.

Finally I found the courage to stand up to him. I yelled at him to back off and leave us alone. I told him that he had to leave Dean's house because they didn't want him there. He laughed at us and disappeared but then came right back. He did this several times, disappearing and then coming back. Whenever he would disappear, the woman and the little girl would come out from behind the boxes, but they would never get too far before he reappeared and they would have to retreat again.

I asked the woman and the little girl why they were there, but they wouldn't answer me. The little girl was whimpering and rubbing her eyes. Her mother tried to console her but didn't seem to have much to give her. I was totally focused on the two of them when someone in the group hollered to me to look out. I whipped around, and the male spirit was right on top of me. He looked so hateful. I yelled at him once again to back off and leave us alone. I said that he was not welcome here and that he had to leave NOW. We said the Lord's Prayer twice and it became very quiet. I no longer saw the mother and daughter, and the man seemed to have left. We sat for a few more minutes to see if this calmness was just temporary or if the ghosts had really gone.

After about five minutes with no more activity, we decided to turn the lights back on, only to discover that the oddest thing had happened. There was a perfectly round puddle of liquid in the middle of our circle. We all kidded each other about who had wet their pants, but no one had, and none of us knew what this liquid was or how it had gotten there. There wasn't a leak in the roof. None of us had brought any water upstairs with us. There just wasn't a logical explanation.

Despite the unexplainable liquid, we felt pretty confident that we had done whatever needed to be done to rid the house of the ghosts, and so we headed downstairs. We were still chatting about everything that had taken place when I started hearing that whimpering sound again. I psychically looked around to see what was going on and, sure enough, there was the little girl.

I psychically asked the mother what was going on, and she said she was really relieved that we had gotten rid of the guy, her husband, because they were very frightened of him. She said that he had murdered them both and then taken his own life, and he would not let any of them go on to the other side. She said they had been there for a long time. When I told her I didn't know what to do for her, she looked so discouraged, and a few seconds later she disappeared. That was the last I saw of any of them.

When we finally left Dean's house that night I was so glad to get out of there. I realized how exhausting this ghostbusting work is, and hoped I wouldn't have to do it too often. Little did I know what I had in store for me.

Ghost Fact

Ghosts can actually feel your fear; they can even breathe it in and grow larger from it. If you are in a fearful situation with a ghost, say a prayer (the Lord's Prayer, for example) that will help you feel at peace and protected. Always ask your guides to protect you. If you feel something close to your face taking your breath away, tell it to back off NOW. Remember, you are more powerful than any entity. When they are breathing in your breath or the energy from your fear, it's just an indication that they are not feeling very powerful and are trying to draw on your power.

A GAGGLE OF GHOSTS

If memory serves me correctly, I didn't get any other calls about ghosts for quite a while. I'm not sure exactly how many years passed between my second encounter with ghosts and my next, but my guess would be about seven.

In the spring of 1980, shortly after our local newspaper, the *Star and Tribune,* ran a feature story on me in the Variety section, I started getting calls for psychic readings and healings coming in from all over the country. My career took off.

I also started getting calls from people who suspected they had ghosts. By this time I had learned quite a bit more about ghosts and felt a lot more confident in my ghostbusting abilities. So when a call came in from a young woman named Martha who said she had moved out of her house because she believed it was overrun with ghosts, I decided to check it out. She said that the house had been on the market for over a year with no interested buyers, and she was sure the ghosts were responsible.

I was intrigued, if a little scared, by all the symptoms she described. Even though I was used to seeing spirits by then, they were usually the friendly type, like spirit guides. Ghosts are a whole different story. They usually have an attitude, and most of the time they aren't real friendly.

By this time my brother, Michael, was doing psychic readings for a career as well. When we were kids, we didn't get along very well because he was always so hyper and I needed a lot of calm around me, but as we got older our personalities seemed to complement each other and we got along really well. He's the comic in the family; I'm the "straight man." I asked him if he would go to Martha's house with me to see if we could find any ghosts. It seemed like a fun thing to do together. It turned out to be quite an experience for both of us.

It was a Sunday evening. My brother and I pulled up in front of a small West St. Paul home. On the outside everything looked normal. A white picket fence surrounded a front yard with hedges that had grown quite tall. The For Sale sign swung in the breeze. The house looked as if it had a fresh coat of white paint on it, and the awnings were trimmed in black. Looking at it from the outside, it seemed hard to believe that this sweet little home in the city could actually be overrun with ghosts.

When we got to the door, Martha told us she had just arrived herself. She seemed a little on edge and told us that she hated coming here, hated the feelings she had while in the house, and really hoped we could do something. She said she had spent hundreds of dollars on exterminators and other professionals, trying to find what was causing the problems, and she was at her wit's end. We sat down in the living room and she introduced us to a friend of hers whom she had brought along. Then we introduced her to Michael's wife, Katie, whom we had brought along. We explained to Martha that the first thing we wanted to do was walk through and get a feel for the place.

Before we get any further, let me explain something about these ghostbusting stories. I realize it's part of my job to create the scene for you so that you can see what I saw as I walked through each experience—that I describe to you what each room looked like, the pictures on the wall, the colors and textures of the furniture, the smells, all the minute details that create these scenes in your mind. The problem is that when we're looking for a ghost, we have to keep the lights down low, for one because it's easier to see ghosts in the dark, but also because our psychic eyes are scoping out the environment on a different dimension. Yes, our human eyes are open and aware of our physical surroundings, but our concentration is elsewhere. So that's where the problem comes in. I often can't remember any details about people's homes! If and when I can, I will certainly share them with you. Now, back to Martha's.

Michael and I opened up psychically, and within seconds we saw our first batch of ghosts. Right in the living room, there was a group of six spirits sitting around a table. They were holding hands, and it looked as if they were praying. Michael and I looked at each other, and he asked me if I could see the spirits sitting at the tables. Yes, I told him, I could. They were very faint and it was hard to make out what they were doing at first, but they had their heads bowed and they were mumbling something.

I asked the spirits what they were doing there, and one of the men told me that they were members of a prayer group that had met at the house every Sunday night when they were living and that they had continued to meet there on Sunday nights since their deaths.

Besides feeling the presence of many other spirits in the house, we could also feel some pretty strong vibes coming from Martha's friend, who clearly thought we were con artists. Michael asked the woman to please wait in the living room while we walked through the house. Looking for ghosts is taxing enough without having to duck someone's negative vibes.

We decided to begin with a small stairway over to the left of the living room that led to the upstairs bedroom. Michael went up first, I followed right behind him, and Katie was behind me. I don't know what prompted me to look behind me, but when I turned around I saw a male ghost with a very snarly, angry look on his face right behind Katie. He put his hands around her neck as if he was going to strangle her. I yelled at him to get away from her and he immediately disappeared. Katie told me she felt something really weird going on around her but had no idea what it was. Although Katie is very sensitive, she has not developed her psychic abilities. She came along with us that night just to see what might happen.

That experience sure freaked us out. Our nerves were starting to get a little raw. Next we spotted the spirits of two small children, a little boy of about five and a four-year-old girl. The little boy had dark hair, sunken-looking eyes, and a pale complexion, and he was dressed in a white shirt and dress pants. The hollowness in his eyes was so sad to see; it looked as if he'd been ill. So I wasn't surprised when, after we asked them what they were doing there, the little boy said he had been sick and after he died he came to this lady's house to play with her toys.

The little girl looked a lot healthier. My guess was that she didn't die from an illness but rather from some kind of accident. She had light-colored hair and was wearing a yellow dress. Her energy was very up. She told us that when she died she came here to play with the little boy so he wouldn't get lonely. They were playing some game and seemed oddly happy, although the energy around them seemed very lonely.

When Michael crouched down to their level to talk with them, the children scurried off into the closet. Then I saw an image of a young male ghost standing right next to Martha's bed. He was about sixteen years old and appeared in leathers that were tattered and torn. He told me he had died in a motorcycle accident in front of this house several years before and had come inside the house instead of going to heaven because he thought it was going to be "really boring over there." He said he loved jumping up and down on Martha's bed and scaring her at night. I got the feeling that he was trying to impress me with how tough he was.

I was feeling pretty overwhelmed by all of the ghosts in this house. All I could think of was, what are were going to do with all of them? I had no clue. I just knew there were more to find, and my energy was already running low. We decided to go down to the kitchen to regroup. We needed to take a little break because being wide open psychically, as you need to be when searching for a ghost, can be exhausting. Fortunately the kitchen was clear of any ghostly entities.

Michael, Katie, and I were sitting at the table for less than a minute when we started to smell the strangest odor. We looked around the kitchen, half hoping to not find whatever was causing the weird stench. The smell led us to the bedroom right off the kitchen, and there on the bed lay a female ghost who actually looked like a skeleton. She was moaning and seemed delirious. Wow, it was so creepy I just wanted out of there. We tried to communicate with her, but she was incoherent. She just kept moaning. She gave off the strongest odor of death. Even Martha's friend the skeptic came in and asked us what the horrible smell was.

Right then and there we just wanted to quit ghosthunting, but we decided to keep going and get the job done. We headed for the basement, where we immediately saw a male and female spirit standing over by the washing machine, talking. Michael asked them who they were and they immediately disappeared. We checked the rest of the basement and found nothing else, so we ventured back upstairs to tell Martha everything we'd found.

Turns out, everything we'd found coincided exactly with the experiences Martha had been having. She said the only room people felt comfortable in was the living room. Sometimes she could hear children giggling in her closet, and some nights she could feel something sit or jump on her bed when she was trying to go to sleep. She said that no matter where she was in the house, she always felt as if a man were watching her. She hated doing the laundry, because there was a spooky feeling by the washing machine. She said she absolutely hated going in the spare bedroom by the kitchen, because she could smell something really weird in there but could never find the source.

We talked for a while about how the ghosts had affected her life. She'd desperately needed someone to talk to who could understand what she was going through. With all the spirit experiences Michael and I had had during our psychic development period, we understood completely.

After Martha seemed to have calmed down, we went back upstairs to begin the process of getting the spirits to move on. We asked our spirit guides to please help us with each situation, and as always they were right there to help.

When we started talking to the sixteen-year-old about going on to the other side, he again told us how boring he thought it would be and said he wanted to stay where he was.

Our guides suggested that we ask the young man if he would take the two children over to heaven. They felt that once the teenager got there, he would see just how wonderful it is and would undoubtedly choose to stay there. We called the children out from the closet and asked the young man if he would assist them to the light, which he agreed to do. He asked us if he could come back once he got them over there, and we told him of course he could (which he could), but we felt pretty confident that he wouldn't be back. And that's exactly how it went.

He took each one of the children by the hand and we talked them through the tunnel as they made their way up the road to the other side. They slowly moved toward the light, and as they moved we could feel all of them let go of their earthly existence. We burned some sage (more about this in the final chapter) to clear out all the fear energy in the room and then went back downstairs.

Martha surprised us when she said that she didn't want us to get rid of the prayer group. She said they actually made her feel good, so we moved on to the spare bedroom. We again asked our guides for assistance, because this old female soul was not paying any attention to us. They suggested asking for an angel to come and take her on to the other side. They said we should explain to her where she was going and tell her that an angel was going to take her there.

Right after we finished explaining this to the sickly woman-ghost, a beautiful female angel came into the room and scooped the woman into her arms. Within thirty seconds, the two of them were floating out of the room. We saw the angel carry her though the tunnel and into the light, which, I must say, was very cool to watch. Again we could feel that sense of release as one more of these earthbound souls let go of life on earth.

We ran downstairs to make sure the man and woman had not come back and found the basement empty. We walked through the house one more time to make sure there were no more spirits hiding anywhere. We burned more sage and asked God to clear and bless the house. Four hours after we had first walked into Martha's house, we were done.

We were all exhausted—mentally, physically, and psychically. We each just wanted to go home, take a shower, wash the vibes off us, and get a good night's sleep; which is exactly what we did, but only after stopping at a fast food drive-thru on our way home. Michael and I had worked up quite an appetite by this point, and had had such an amazing experience that we had a lot to talk about. Working together was great, and it was very validating for both of us that we always saw the same things. We were learning so much about ghosts and how to get them over to the other side, which was really cool. We talked about how scared we felt at certain times and how at other times we didn't feel any fear. We could see that we could really be of some help to people, and that felt good.

About two weeks later, we called Martha to see how everything was going. She said she had moved back into the house the next day and hadn't experienced any of the old ghost symptoms. She told us that the house had sold the following weekend and that she and her brother had gotten the price they had originally asked for. She was so happy, and so were we.

After Martha's house was cleared, word spread that we had the ability to get rid of ghosts, and we started getting calls from other people with haunted houses. Slowly we became known around Minneapolis and St. Paul as the brother/sister ghostbusting team. We started getting invitations to appear on different television and radio shows and were written about in lots of magazines and newspapers. We couldn't believe how our careers were taking off because of people's fascination with ghosts!

We've never counted or kept track of our clients, so I can only guesstimate that over the last twenty years we've gone into well over one hundred homes and dealt with hundreds of ghosts. Michael and I don't always work together, though we like to when our schedules permit. Sometimes I take along a student who is interested in learning about ghostbusting, and once in a great while, I'll go by myself—if the job doesn't sound too scary!

My ghostbusting stories are as varied as the ghosts that they are about. It all boils down to being good at dealing with all sorts of people . . . only these people just happen to be dead!

Ghost Fact

When there are child ghosts in a house, we've found it works very well to ask one of the adult ghosts, often the one most resistant, to escort the children to the light and through to the other side. We tell the children to hold hands so that none of them wander off as they make their way through the tunnel.

THE GHOST WHO HATED CHILDREN

Not all ghosts are here to make trouble, but once in a while we find one who's just downright mean. A young couple called and told us that their two small children, ages three and four, were complaining that there was a "mean man" in their bedroom who was trying to push them down the stairs. The mom said that she wasn't sure if there really was something there but that she was concerned because the children were afraid to be in their room and wouldn't stop talking about this man.

We decided it would be best to do this job when the children were asleep so as not to call any more attention to the situation. We went over to their home at about nine o'clock that night. We could tell immediately that this couple was nervous. The woman kept apologizing for asking us to come over, and the man told us he didn't think there was anything there. He just thought the kids had overactive imaginations.

As we explained to them how we did our work, my brother and I were both psychically scanning the house for any indication of earthbound spirits. There was definitely a *feeling* of a ghost somewhere, listening to our conversation. It was just one of those feelings when you *know* something's up, and we were anxious to find out what it was. First we checked out the living room and dining room. No ghosts. The husband's home office had a lot of tense energy in it, but it too was clear of ghosts. But when we got to the kitchen, it started to feel creepy. I didn't like it at all. We could feel angry male vibes in there, and we could tell they weren't the vibes of anyone who physically lived in the house. The energy felt old and stale, which usually indicates that there's a ghost somewhere around the area.

We began to head up the stairs to the bedrooms, and I suddenly felt gripped with fear. I could see a presence slowly beginning to form at the top of the stairs. I told Michael I didn't think I could go up there because it was really creeping me out. He told me to wait in the kitchen. He said he would bring the ghost downstairs because he wanted to talk with him without waking up the kids.

I stood at the bottom of the stairs and watched Michael walk to the top of the stairs and begin talking to the ghost. He asked him what his name was, and the ghost answered,

"Roy." Michael asked Roy why he was here in this home, and Roy told him he liked the house—well actually he liked the adults but hated the kids and just wanted them out of there. He said that he tried several times to push them down the stairs, and that he really liked scaring them. When Michael told Roy that we had come to get him to go on to the other side, I could feel him becoming very angry.

Then something happened that I had never seen before. The hallway filled up with a very thick, gray energy, almost like a fog. It was so thick that I couldn't see my brother. I called to him and asked him if he was all right. His voice was very soft, but he told me not to worry. I kept telling him to talk to me, tell me what was going on, but for several minutes—probably four or five in all—he said nothing. My guides told me to stay downstairs, that this ghost was just filled with hatred and that I didn't need to feel it. They reassured me that Michael was okay, although I had my doubts. My big fear was that this Roy had entered Michael's body and that was why he wasn't answering. But just as I was about to go upstairs and get him, I heard Michael tell Roy to go downstairs because he wanted to talk to him away from the children.

When they got down to the kitchen, I was surprised to see how fragile Roy appeared. He was a little under six feet tall, with light brown hair and eyes that were sunken in. He had this really awful gray aura and looked very thin, like skin and bones (strange way to describe a ghost, I know, but he had that malnourished look, which, believe it or not, not all ghosts share).

I asked Roy why he hadn't gone on to the other side, and he said that his parents had been very abusive to him when he was living and that he didn't want to go anywhere where they might be. He was so adamant about it; I didn't think we were ever going to get him to go over to the light. We asked our guides for some help, and they came up with a brilliant suggestion. They told us that when Roy was alive he had had a dog named Copper whose soul now resided on the other side. They said they would go get Copper and bring him to this room, and we should tell Roy that if he wanted to be with Copper he would have to go over to the other side with him. They also said to reassure him that he would not have to come in contact with his parents.

Our guides left the room to get the dog, and Michael asked Roy if he had had a dog when he was living. Yes, he said, he had owned a golden retriever named Copper. Right about then the dog's soul came leaping into the room, and Roy was down on the ground, hugging and kissing him. The dog was as excited to see him as he was to see the dog.

We told Roy that if he wanted to hang out with Copper he would have to go on to the other side, because that is where the dog lived. We both reassured him that he would not have to see his parents. We told him to just tell the greeters on the other side that he did not want to see his parents, and it would be all right. We could see that he was really struggling with the decision; he hated his parents with a passion, but his love for Copper convinced him to go.

We watched as the two of them floated through the tunnel and into the light. What an incredible experience. We both knew that animals have souls and go on to the other side, but we'd never had an animal be a part of a ghostbusting job before. We went back into the living room and told the young couple what we had found. We reassured them that the ghost was gone. Before leaving, we burned some sage and walked through the house one more time, asking that it be cleared of all negative vibes. We advised the couple not to say much to the children other than to tell them that the man was now gone and they were safe. We also warned them not to talk about the ghost while in the house for the next three days, because we had learned the hard way that if people talk a lot about their ghost right after a ghostbusting, the ghost can hear them from the other side and get the impression that he is missed. In some cases, the ghost has actually returned.

After we left, Michael and I sat in the van for at least five minutes and just stared out the window. I asked Michael what he was doing upstairs in that gray hazy energy, and he explained that he just sat there so he could feel Roy's energy and what it felt like to be Roy. He said it was a cold, dead nothingness, and he was real glad to be done with the job. As usual, we headed for a fast food restaurant before going home. We cranked up the radio to get us grounded back here on earth and chatted about everything under the sun *but ghosts.*

Ghost Fact

Children and animals can see ghosts and spirits easily because their intellect isn't getting in the way, telling them it's not possible. If your dog growls or your cat hisses at nothing, or your children talk to "nothing," chances are you have a ghost or a visiting spirit.

THE GHOST WHO
WAS AFRAID OF GOD

In my psychic development classes, our teacher taught us that all suicide victims go to a place in between our plane and the other side, called limbo, where they remain until the natural time of their death would have occurred. When we went on our next ghostbusting job, I was glad to find out that that information did not apply to all souls who commit suicide.

My mom got a call from a treatment center in Minneapolis that had formerly been a funeral parlor. They were doing a lot of reconstruction on the building, and the workers were complaining about a certain part of the building that was giving them the willies. Apparently, some very strange noises were coming from an old elevator shaft that had been boarded up for years. Workers also complained that their tools were being moved around and said they felt as if something or someone was watching them.

Mom asked Michael and me if we would go check it out because the owners were friends of hers and she was concerned about them. When we first arrived, we did our usual walk-through, just to see what we could find. There were definitely a lot of spirits floating around the place. There were three in particular who appeared out of nowhere and came looming at us really fast, as if to purposely try to scare us. I must admit they had my heart pounding for a few minutes. I'm used to ghosts trying to hide from us, not looming towards us. Turns out they were teenage ghosts, all dressed in black leather. They were quite obnoxious. They yelled and laughed and generally tried to scare us out of there.

We saw ghosts hiding behind plants and others roaming the halls. We made our way up to the third floor, and that's when we came upon the boarded-up elevator shaft. Psychically, Michael and I could both see the soul of a young man who appeared to be hanging from a beam inside the shaft. We looked at each other, wanting confirmation from the other that we were both seeing this. We walked closer to the elevator and asked the young man what his name was, how old he was, and why he was in there.

He told us his name was John and that he had hanged himself at the age of twenty-one. He appeared to be quite emotional, as if he had been crying. We asked him why he didn't go on to the other side, and he said he was afraid to go to heaven because he thought God was mad at him for taking his own life. I asked my guides about the whole idea of him going to limbo, and they said that that information wasn't accurate. Suicide victims can go into heaven like everyone else, they said, but a lot of times they don't feel worthy of going because they have taken their own lives, so they just find someplace here and stay stuck.

We told the young man that he could go into heaven, and he said he didn't believe us, so we asked our guides if they had any suggestions as to how to help him. They suggested that they go to the other side and bring his parents (both deceased) to this place. They said maybe the parents could convince him to go home with them. We asked our guides if they would please find them for us, at which point they left the room. It was about thirty seconds later that our guides and John's parents came floating into the area. They floated right up to John and the three of them hugged. It was quite an emotional scene. They told John that God wasn't angry with him for taking his own life and that he had suffered enough in this elevator shaft. They said he was welcome to come home with them and told him about other relatives who were anxious to see him again. He looked at us and asked if all of this was for real, and we told him, yes, it was. He was quite anxious about whether or not he was doing the right thing, but after a few minutes of thinking it over, he left with his parents and we watched them all float into white light.

We both felt so good about what had just happened that it made the rest of the job go a lot easier. We made our way through the rest of the treatment center and cleared out the remaining twelve ghosts.

Ghost Fact

Many times we have found a ghost so filled with remorse, guilt, or shame about something it did during its lifetime that it is completely stuck. The ghost won't allow itself to go on. Deceased loved ones do come and try to get these ghosts to come home with them, but many feel they must stay here in a state of limbo and be punished. The truth is, they are the ones who condemn themselves to limbo, but they can set themselves free whenever they're ready to.

THE GHOST WHO WAS IN LOVE

About ten years ago I received a call from a realtor who said that a house he was trying to sell had been on the market for several months and all the prospective buyers seemed frightened before they even got in the front door. Some would turn around and leave without going inside. Michael wasn't able to go this time, so I took along my good friend, Mike Warnell.

As Mike and I walked through the house, I couldn't see anything, but I could feel someone watching me from the third floor. As I approached the master bedroom on the third floor, I could feel an angry, cold energy standing around the corner. I had chills all over my body.

I walked into the bedroom and there he was: a male ghost standing on the side of the bed where the woman of the house slept. In my dialogue with the ghost, he told me that his name was Bob and that he was in love with the woman who lived there. He didn't want her to move! I had already discovered that ghosts don't usually move with people when they move out of a house, because they tend not to like (or are frightened of) change. To keep his beloved from moving out, Bob had taken to standing by the front door to frighten anyone who came to see the house.

Ghosts can become as obsessed with people as people can, and this ghost thought he was very much in love with this woman. The woman then told me that she had had a couple of dreams about some man who was interested in her. In one dream, her wedding ring was removed and put on top of the bookshelf. When she woke up the next morning, she found that her ring was off. Because the shelf was so high, she had to get a chair to stand on in order to see if the ring was on the top shelf—and it was. There was no way this woman could have done all of that in her sleep.

My guides directed me to have the woman tell Bob that she loved her husband and wanted Bob to leave her alone and go to the other side NOW. She did this, and I talked to Bob about letting go and moving through the tunnel. He said he was lonely and wanted to be in love. I reassured him that he could find a relationship on the other side. He seemed relieved to hear this and said he was willing to give it a try. I directed him to look for the light and move toward it, which he did. After seeing him go into the light, I saged the house from top to bottom to get rid of all the negative energy in there.

Before leaving, I reminded the homeowners not to talk about Bob for a few days while in the house, lest he think he was missed and come back. I called about a week later to see how everything was going, and the couple had already sold the house. They asked if I would go check out their new house to make sure Bob hadn't gone over there. I did go, and he hadn't. He remained on the other side.

Ghost Fact

Many ghosts can be romantics, too. Sometimes a ghost gets really attached to someone on this side and can't let go. If you think a ghost may be smitten with you, be very direct and tell it to move on. If you're serious and it can sense it, it will move on.

THE GHOST WHO WAS AFRAID OF HER SISTER

A good friend of mine and I were driving up around northern Minnesota one fall day, just going from town to town exploring the area via the back roads. At some point, from the road, we could see the top of an old house back in the woods and decided to go investigate. The dirt road that led to the house was almost grown over with weeds. As we got closer, I could see a faint image of an older woman ghost standing in the window on the second floor. She was just standing there looking out the window as if she were in a trance, just a blank stare on her face. She noticed that I was watching her and ducked back from the window. My friend stopped the car and suggested we go inside. I'm usually pretty chicken about things like this—I'm the one who worries that the sheriff will pull up and arrest me for trespassing. But I decided to take a risk and go check out the ghost.

The front door was wide open, so we walked right in. The place was filthy. There was fifties-era wallpaper on the walls that was half torn down, old broken-down furniture, and torn curtains in some of the windows. Lots of cigarette butts all over the floor, too, and holes in the wood floors. I could feel the presence of young people in the building, as if it was a hangout for teenagers. I wanted to get out of there because it smelled so bad, but I kept feeling pulled upstairs. I was also curious to find out if there really was an older woman spirit standing near the window.

I didn't mention anything about the ghost to my friend, just in case I was imagining it. A part of me was hoping she wasn't there because I wasn't in the mood for ghosts. I wanted to play, not work, but I felt an obligation to at least see if there was a stuck soul upstairs. I told my friend we needed to check out the upstairs, and he rolled his eyes but followed me up.

Up we went and there she was, standing in a bedroom all by herself. She looked to be about eighty-five years old, white-haired and frail. I slowly approached her and asked her what her name was and why she was here in this old abandoned house. She didn't give me her name but told me that she used to live nearby, and when she died she decided she did not want to go to heaven, because she didn't want to see her sister. She said her sister had always been terribly mean to her when they were living and that she had been so relieved when her sister had died. Then, when she herself died, she didn't know what to do to avoid her sister, so she decided to take refuge in the abandoned house. She said the house she used to live in no longer existed, so she found this one and stayed.

I asked her if she knew what year it was, and she didn't have a clue. I asked her if she could remember what year she died. Nope, couldn't remember. She told me she had never married.

I asked her if there were other deceased members of her family in the house, but she just stared out the broken window again, as if she were back in a trance. I told her I thought she should move on into the light and start a new life for herself. She looked at me with a blank stare. Then she asked me two questions that I had never been asked by a ghost: Could she wear pink in heaven, and could she get her hair done there? I told her I didn't see why not.

Then she asked what she would do about her sister. I told her heaven was a big place and that there would be angels who would help her over to the other side if she wanted their help. All she needed to do was tell them she did not want to see her sister. Again she asked whether she could get her hair done there, and again I told her I didn't think it would be a problem. She agreed to go.

I asked my guides if they would get an angel to come and help her over to the other side, which they did. I talked her though the tunnel, even though the angel was with her. I could sense that she needed the reassurance. It took about five minutes total, but she did go into the light.

Later on, I asked my guides if they had directed us to that old house. They just smiled.

Ghost Fact

There are lots of stuck souls here on earth who simply do not want to go on to the other side and face certain people from their lifetime. It's much better to do what you can before dying in the way of forgiveness and amends so that you don't end up a soul hiding out on earth.

THE GHOST
WHO WAS A COP

One November, on a rainy Sunday afternoon, I got a call from a very frantic young woman who said she was the owner of a massage parlor in Minneapolis and that some very strange things were happening there. She said they were experiencing banging on the walls and could feel someone watching them. She told me that there had been an incident the night before where *something* had ripped the shower curtain off the rod when one of their "johns" was taking a shower. The man had grabbed his clothes and run out of there. I told her I would come check it out that night.

When I got there I found a lounge area, where I met two of the masseuses. They were very nice young women who were obviously frightened by the events taking place in the building. I could see into several massage rooms, each softly lit, with a massage table and some oil. On this particular evening there were no customers, so I just roamed the halls looking for the ghost. Was I ever surprised to round one corner and come face to face with a male ghost dressed in a policeman's uniform! He told me his name was Bill and that he had died three years earlier near the parlor. I asked him if he knew about the tunnel and the white light and he said that, yes, he was familiar with both. He said that several of his deceased relatives had come to try to convince him to come over to the other side, but for now he chose to remain on this side and protect the girls.

Bill said that when he banged on the walls, it was a sign to the girls that they needed to beware of a particular patron who was not safe. Then he asked me to tell the owner that he was sorry about ripping the shower curtain off the rod last night, but that he'd really lost his temper when he realized that the John in the shower was a priest. When I told her what he'd said, she was convinced that I'd seen her ghost. How else would I have known about the priest?

Through me, Bill asked if he could please stay and continue to protect the girls. He said the banging on the wall was not to frighten them but to protect them. The owner had joined us by this time. The girls took a vote and unanimously decided to keep Bill around. Bill assured me that when he was ready to move on, he would go into the light.

Ghost Fact

Souls will sometimes stick around if they're older and genuinely concerned for people on this side, or younger but using that as an excuse. We can always tell if the concern is genuine or not, but in either case, we reassure the ghost that there are many people on this side who can help these people out. The ghost needs to learn to let go and trust that people will take care of themselves or find others to help them.

THE GHOSTS WHO
WERE STONED

One day, Michael and I were called to the home of a young woman who was terrified to sleep in her bedroom. She said she could feel something watching her every night. She had wanted to call us for some time, but her landlord didn't want her to. She said he didn't believe in ghosts and thought we were just scam artists. After many discussions about this, the landlord agreed to let her hire us to do her room only, but we were to leave the rest of the house alone.

It was a beautiful home in the wealthier part of Minneapolis. Built in the early 1900s, it had all the original woodwork, elegant staircases, big stone fireplaces, and original chandeliers. At first, it was fun to walk through this very regal-looking home, but once we opened up psychically we saw a whole different picture. The place was crawling with ghosts, and there was something very odd about them. We didn't know what was going on at first, so we just kept moving through the house. We met the landlord, who seemed like a nice guy. Although outwardly he acted as if he believed in what we did, we could feel his skepticism. As we sat in the kitchen talking with him, the oddest thing happened. We started seeing spirits go in and out of him. At first I thought I was seeing things, but when I asked Michael about it, he said he saw it too. We kept watching to get a better understanding of what was going on, and then one of my guides told me that this man smoked a lot of pot and that the spirits would go in and out of him throughout the day to have the experience of being high. Now it made sense to us that he didn't want us to do any of the other rooms. He was being heavily influenced by these drugged spirits and wanted to be left alone.

When we were finally alone with our client again, we asked her if the landlord smoked pot, and she said, "Oh yeah, all day." We asked her if his personality changed much, and she said, "All the time." At that point there weren't too many spirits in her room, but there was definitely a feeling that these spirits did not respect people's boundaries and would probably wander into her room whenever they felt like it.

We did a general ghostbusting. We told all the spirits that were in our client's room to leave and to stay out. We heavily saged the room, and then we visualized sealing the room in a white light, which, according our guides, sets up an outer boundary so spirits know to not come in. It was hard for both of us to leave that day, knowing that the landlord was being possessed regularly and that the house was filled with stoned ghosts, but we had to respect his wishes. It did not feel right to say anything to him about what we had observed. This was how he liked living his life.

I talked to the client a couple of weeks later, and she reported that the difference between her room and the rest of the house was so significant that she was thinking of moving out. She said she really liked the energy in her room, which had remained clear, and wanted to go find a place to live that had that feeling all throughout.

Ghost Fact

Souls who had a drug or alcohol problem when they were living may choose to hang out with people who have a similar addiction and may actually take over their bodies from time to time in order to still feel that high. If you are a heavy drinker, alcoholic, or drug addict, ask God or your spirit guides to protect your body from these entities—especially when you're intoxicated.

THE GHOST WHO WAS THROWING THE RENTER AROUND

Every time I think I've learned everything there is to know about ghosts, I get a call that leaves me speechless. In the summer of 1991, we received a call from a woman who rented out several rooms in her house to men. She said that some very unbelievable things were going on in her house. One of her renters, Tom, a man well over six feet tall, was being attacked by a ghost every once in a while. She was afraid to tell him that she'd called us, because she was afraid he would get mad, but we asked her to please have him there when we arrived so we could ask him some questions and make sure this was for real.

We had some difficulty setting this up. Every time we made an appointment with them, they canceled it. Finally the third appointment was a go. Our client asked her renter,

Tom, to be at our meeting at six o'clock. At seven fifteen, he came strolling through the front door with a real attitude. He wouldn't even look at us. Strangely, until he got there we hadn't seen any ghost activity at all, but within minutes of his arrival, Michael and I both saw a female ghost standing down the hall by Tom's room. She was standing around the corner thinking we couldn't see her.

Slowly Tom began to tell us what was going on. He said there was a female spirit around the house who had a crush on him. Whenever he brought a woman home to his room, the female spirit would become really jealous and start slapping him in the face. According to him, there were a few times when she picked him up and threw him into the walls. Imagine, here's this six-foot-three-inch man looking at me, telling me that this female ghost picks him up and throws him into the walls when he brings a woman home. I'm sure my mouth was hanging wide open. I looked at my brother for an explanation, but he looked as perplexed as I felt.

Turns out the man was really upset with his landlady for interfering. He liked this ghost. He told us he thought it was kind of cute the way she threw him around and that he wanted to keep her. He told his landlady that if she insisted on having us get rid of the ghost, he would move out. It seemed very clear that these two people needed to figure out what they wanted to do. We told them to call us if they decided together to get rid of the ghost, because if we tried to do it at the landlady's request, Tom could always call his ghost friend back from the light. We never heard from them again.

Ghost Fact

Some people think of their ghosts as pets, and what's sad is that these souls often think of themselves as pets. They're grateful to be loved, no matter where it comes from. When we run into this type of situation, we talk to the ghost about going to the other side and developing some real relationships with other souls. We tell it that it deserves better than to be someone's pet. These ghosts usually have very low self-esteem, so we are gentle and loving toward them. But it is also important to be firm about the fact that they need to set themselves free and begin a new way of having relationships. Ghosts are people, not pets.

THE GHOST WHO DIDN'T KNOW HE WAS DEAD

This was one of those jobs that completely took me by surprise. Up to that point, all the ghosts I had encountered knew they were dead, but this young man seemed to have no idea. One chilly fall evening in 1986, I was called to a house near the University of Minnesota campus. A young woman had called saying that something was knocking books off bookshelves and jumping up and down on her bed. Also, things were being moved from room to room. Clothes had been thrown out of the closet and onto the floor. She said she was afraid to come home every day for fear of what would happen next.

When I walked into her bedroom, I immediately saw the ghost of a young man in an army uniform with blood all over the front of it. I asked him what his name was and why he was there. He said his name was Kenneth and he was there to get his house back. He said he had come back from Vietnam and this woman was living in his house. I asked him what year he thought it was. He said 1968. He told me he'd done everything he could to get this b___h out of his house, but that she wouldn't go. I asked him if he knew he was dead, and he argued that if he was dead I wouldn't be talking to him.

He went into a rage, yelling at me to get out of the house and leave him alone. "Take this b___h with you, too" he said. My first reaction was to yell back, but instead I decided to approach him gently and talk to him calmly about his situation. Kenneth obviously needed help accepting his death. It looked as though he had died in Vietnam. His memory was very fuzzy. All he remembered was going off to war and then being back here in Minneapolis, trying to get back into his house.

When I told Kenneth that he needed to accept that his physical body had died, he appeared to start crying. (Yes, souls do release their emotions through crying, but their tears aren't wet!) He told me he didn't want to be dead, that he was only twenty years old. He alternated between being really angry and really sad. He must have told me at least a half a dozen times that he wasn't dead and to get the hell out of his house. We went around and around about why he should move on to the other side and why I wouldn't make my client leave instead. Sometimes during our conversation he would disappear and then reappear again.

It was a long two and a half hours before something shifted and Kenneth became willing to go through the tunnel to the other side. I just kept telling him he deserved to be free. He was young and could make a fresh start for himself. I asked him if he could remember family members or friends from Nam who had passed away. He said that he remembered a couple of buddies who had died in the war. I told him he could see them again if he went over, and that seemed to bring some comfort to him. Reluctantly, Kenneth moved into the tunnel and toward the white light. He thanked me just before taking his first step into the light.

As usual, I instructed the young woman who lived in the house not to talk about the ghost for few days, because he would be able to hear her and might get the impression she wanted him back.

Three days later, I got a phone call from the woman's roommate. She said that Kenneth was back. The roommate told me that the woman had really missed Kenneth and had asked him to return. The roommate told me that if things got really crazy again, he was going to move out. I never heard from either of them again. I guess this young woman realized that she would rather live with Kenneth than without him.

Ghost Fact

Sometimes if a person doesn't believe in life after death, he will not move on to the other side when he dies, because he won't understand what's going on. He will simply hang out in a place most familiar to him here on earth. Sometimes when loved ones from the other side come to the aid of these earth-bound spirits, they think they're just hallucinating. The good news is, most people do believe in some kind of afterlife, so this doesn't happen that often.

When you're dealing with souls who don't believe they're dead, it's important to be honest and direct and tell them that their physical body is dead and that there is a very special place for them to go. We tell them to look for the light, and we strongly encourage them to move toward it. We tell them that their deceased loved ones are in this special place and that they will be reunited with them as soon as they get there. We repeat this several times so that they really get that we're not some kind of hallucination, and that this is all for real.

THE GHOST WHO KEPT HIS CHILDREN AWAY

An hour after I got a call from a producer at NBC's *The Other Side* wanting to know if I had any interesting ghostbusting jobs coming up, I got a call from a man in south Minneapolis who was really upset because his children were afraid to sleep at his house. He explained that his nine-year-old daughter, Samantha, was complaining of a creepy feeling in the house, and his fourteen-year-old son, Daniel, was seeing and hearing spirits in the house. Daniel could apparently hear children spirits playing in the attic, bouncing a ball and laughing, and could also see an angry male soul roaming the halls of their beautiful home. The final straw for the dad was the day he ran out to his car to get something, and when he got back to the house something or someone had locked the front door from the inside. But no one was home but him!

I asked him if he would be willing to be on TV, and he said he was open to doing whatever he had to so that his kids would be comfortable staying over again. It turned out to be a really fun show. The camera crew was great, and Dr. Will, the show's host at the time, came to Minneapolis and slept in Daniel's haunted bedroom. The show hired a sketch artist, Paul Johnson, and also invited Dale Kaczmarek, the president of the Ghost Research Society, to join us with all of his electronic equipment that measures ghost activity.

The attic was quite different than I'd expected. It had been completely renovated and was really beautiful— white carpeting, all new windows, walls painted white, skylights in the ceiling. A regulation pool table sat in the middle. There was a big-screen TV off to the side, with a beautiful leather couch across from it. The father told me he had had the attic completely redone, hoping his kids would enjoy coming over, and he was angry that the ghosts were interfering with their lives.

As I walked around the attic, I could see six children ghosts on one side of the billiard table, sitting in a circle playing with a ball. Ghosts can manifest the same kinds of objects we have here, simply by thinking of them. They are invisible to us because they are not made of matter, but they are visible to other ghosts—and to me. If children ghosts want to play with a ball, they simply think of one and they have one.

I walked over and sat down on the floor, so as to be right at their level, and asked the ghost children who they were and why they were there. One by one, they gave me their names, first names only: Annie spoke first, then Dougy, Timmy, Susy, Connie, and Marky. Annie said they all lived in a house "over there," pointing in a direction west of the house. I asked her if they were related to each other, and she said no, that they were not related, but they had lived together, gotten sick, and died around the same time. I asked her why they didn't go on to the other side, and she said they didn't want to, they just wanted to play. They didn't want to grow up.

One by one, each child drifted out of the house. I asked Annie where they were going, and she said that they played at other houses in the neighborhood too. I asked her if they would all come back later, and she said yes, they would. Just as she was leaving, she told me to watch out for the mean guy who lived downstairs. I wasn't sure if she was talking about the owner or a spirit, but since the owner was a pretty nice guy, I figured she was referring to a spirit. When I shared all this with the owner of the house, he nodded, saying he'd been told there used to be an orphanage just down the road that had burned down.

Once all the children were out of the attic, we moved downstairs to look for the angry spirit that Annie spoke about. I found him sitting in the TV room off to the side of the living room. He was more than six feet tall, with dark hair and eyes, and he had a scowl on his face. I asked him what his name was and why he was there. He said his name was Roger and that this was his house. I asked him if he had been a previous owner of the home, and he said that he could never have afforded this house, but that now that he was dead, he had moved in and taken over. He talked about how lonely he was and told me he enjoyed scaring the little kids in the attic. Then he moved out of the room and disappeared.

I walked through the rest of the house—all four floors of it—and in a closet in the basement found a ghost named Elmer. He seemed disoriented and spoke somewhat incoherently about his wife, Rose, wondering where she was. It seemed like he had Alzheimer's or something. He was very confused about his existence. I asked my guides for help, and they said they would go get Rose, but that I needed to talk to Elmer and help him understand that he was dead. My guides went and got Rose from the other side and brought her back to Elmer. Theirs was one of those sweet reunions where all it took was getting them back together to get the stuck one to move to the other side.

My guides told me that Rose had been there to get Elmer before, but he didn't understand what was going on and wouldn't leave with her. Once I could see that the two of them were in the light, we moved back upstairs to try to find Roger again. He was sitting over on the piano bench in the front room.

I showed Dale Kaczmarek where Roger was sitting, and he put his "ghost meter" on top of the piano. It definitely registered ghost activity. This gadget had ten lights on it; depending on how much ghost energy there was in the room, a different number of lights would light up. This time I think about six lights lit up. We were all quite impressed.

I asked my guides what to do with Roger because he was such a crabby guy. They suggested that Daniel be the one to tell Roger to go on to the other side. Daniel could see him and had seen him roaming the halls of this big house many times. Roger liked scaring Daniel. It just seemed right for all concerned that Daniel be the one to tell Roger that he was not welcome and that he needed to move on to the other side. Roger asked me if it was possible to find a relationship on the other side, and I told him yes, definitely! That got his attention. Both Daniel and I urged him to move through the tunnel into the light, and after arguing with us for a while about why he shouldn't have to go, he finally did leave.

It was now around eleven o'clock and we were all getting tired. We had been ghosthunting for hours. When you do a TV show like this, you have to set up the camera equipment and all the lighting in the room you are going to shoot the scene in, and then move it all to the next room. It can take many hours just to shoot an hour's worth of film. We had been at it since about three o'clock that afternoon. We still needed to go back up to the attic and see if we could pick up any ghost activity on Dale's equipment from the children.

When we got there, all six of them were there, playing with their ball. They were cute all right, but they looked so drawn, so blank in the eyes, as if there was very little life in their little souls. I had no idea how long it had been since they'd died, and they didn't seem to know either.

Dale set up his equipment on the floor near the area where the children were playing. One by one the children came over to see what was going on. As the children got close to the machine, the lights on the meter went up to five or six. We put a red ball on the floor and the producer had me ask the children if they would move the ball. They tried, to no avail. It's just not that easy, especially with energy as low as theirs was. They tried several times to get the ball to move, but it just wasn't happening. Their little hands kept going right through it.

I asked the children to gather around because I wanted to talk to them about going away. I told them that going to the other side didn't mean they had to grow up. I said that there was a lot to do over there and a lot of toys and fun things to play with. I encouraged them to take each other's hands and move into the tunnel and toward the light.

Dougy seemed to be the most mature, so I asked him if he would be the leader and take them over. He was so sweet and said yes, he would do that. They all held hands, and I coaxed them through the tunnel. I kept telling them they were doing a good job and to just keep going. Finally they were at the light. I told them not to be afraid, that they were going to be very happy there. I urged Dougy to just keep going, right through that light, which is exactly what they did. What a rewarding day.

For those of you wondering how Dr. Will's night in the haunted bedroom went, the next morning he reported that he'd slept like a baby!

Ghost Fact

Oftentimes it's better that the owner or resident of a house tell the ghost to leave and go toward the light. It's empowering to the resident to know he can make this happen, and it gives the message loud and clear to the ghost that it is not wanted.

THE GHOSTS
IN THE WOODS

It was the summer of 1993. I had taken time off from ghostbusting for a few months because I had grown weary of arguing with souls who wanted to stay stuck. My brother's life was going in one direction, raising his two children, and mine was going in another—I was teaching classes three nights a week and seeing four clients a day for healings. As full as my plate was, I couldn't resist when I got a call from the TV show *Sightings* wanting to know if I would fly to Colorado Springs and identify some ghosts for a segment they were doing on hauntings. I always learned so much from the ghost stories that the TV shows came up with, and they were just fun to do.

The producers told me that the only problem was that these ghosts only came out at night, and they wondered if I'd mind working from midnight to morning. Sounded intriguing. I was scheduled to teach two workshops the same day they wanted me to fly out, but there was no other time we could all do it, so I decided to just look at it as an adventure. It had been a while since I'd been up all night!

It was a very hot day in mid-July. I did the two workshops, raced home, took a shower, and headed for the airport at about six o'clock that night. I arrived in Denver around ten-thirty. We were held up in the air for a while because there was a violent thunderstorm going on. It was pretty eerie—lightning all throughout the sky, rain pouring down. I remember thinking how perfect the weather was for filming a spooky segment for television, with all that thunder and lightning crashing in the background.

Scott, the owner of the haunted log cabin, was at the airport to pick me up. He was very open about not believing in ghosts. He said he didn't know what it was that had taken over his house, but that he certainly didn't believe in disembodied spirits. He was from Louisiana and had a strong Southern drawl. As we drove through several towns in Colorado with the thunderstorm pounding outside of the car, I listened to him tell me story after story about some of the things that went on in his house: beams of light coming through the house, UFO sightings near his property, police confiscating photographs he showed them and then claiming they had never seen them. He said that he and his wife Bev would lie in bed at night and watch a light show of different colors on the ceiling. They heard chains rattling around in their house. At times they heard voices, other times footsteps. Things moved from room to room. He and his wife had decided to install surveillance cameras inside their house to take pictures of all the activity.

It took close to an hour to get to their house up in the mountains. It was a big, beautiful, rustic log cabin. A fog hung about ten feet above the ground. There were no streetlights or stars to light the pitch-black sky.

When I entered the three-story log cabin, I was quickly greeted by the producer, who asked if I would mind having a seat while the scientist they had hired told us about his ThermaCam. It was a very expensive camera that was used to measure the intensity of heat in a room. The theory was that the ThermaCam might pick up ghost activity because ghosts are cold and would register on the camera. I was more than glad to just sit and relax for a while. It was close to midnight and I was starting to get a little tired.

No sooner had I sat down when a voice behind me said, "Hey, hey, over here." I turned around, and to my right there was a male ghost. He seemed to be about six feet tall, and was wearing blue jeans and a blue checked flannel shirt. He smiled at me and I sent a thought back to him to please be quiet because I wanted to hear what the scientist was saying. Well he didn't care, because he just kept saying, "Hey, hey, look over here." Then I heard it in unison. I turned around again, and now there were five male spirits, all dressed alike, except that each one had a different-colored flannel shirt on.

The original ghost said his name was Tom and told me that this was his house and that no one was going to make him go to the other side. He ran the show around here and had for a long time. I hurriedly told the producer what was happening just in case he wanted to get our dialogue on tape, which he did. The producer set me up with a microphone, and the conversation began. Tom told us why he and the boys felt they deserved to stay in the house. This was his land, his home, and he was not willing to leave it. He said he was a lot like Scott, the new owner. He talked about Scott and Bev for a while and gave me quite an earful on the history of the area.

The cameraman, to whom I had not yet been introduced, asked me if these guys were responsible for knocking his very expensive equipment off the countertop. All five ghosts answered with a resounding "Yes" and then disappeared completely out of sight. Meanwhile, the scientist, Ted, had turned on his ThermaCam, and we did record on film the drop in temperature in exactly the spot where Tom had stood.

We decided to walk through the house to see what else I might find. There in the living room over by the big picture window were three more male spirits. They looked as though they had all just come in from a fishing trip. None of them would talk—they just stared at each other. I tried two or three times to get a conversation going, but to no avail. They just didn't want to talk. Two or three minutes later, they disappeared.

The producer asked Bev if she would show me some of the photographs of the ghosts they had taken over the years. He was curious to see my reaction. We sat at the kitchen table, and just as we started looking through the photo albums, some dogs outside started barking. It was somewhere between one and two in the morning, so it seemed strange that anyone would be outside, but the dogs would not stop barking.

In order to be able to pick up sound on the microphones, the camera crew needed to quiet the dogs down, so the producer went outside to see what was wrong. When he opened up the door, a huge, ten-foot white mass of energy came into the house. Of course no one could see it but me.

A voice within this white mass told me that "they" lived in the forest and that they didn't come into the house very often, but they were curious to see what all the commotion was about. They had seen lights set up around the outside of the house (the crew had put them there to create a scary effect) and the vans and cars parked outside, so I guess it was reasonable that they would wonder what was going on. I told the producer about the white haze, and Bev asked me if it looked anything like this one photo that had been taken by their surveillance camera.

She showed me the photo, and yes, it was exactly the same. Actually, I was in awe of this beautiful white energy. I explained to the voice within the mass that this was a television crew, taping a segment for a TV show. He simply said, "Oh, okay," and out of the log cabin the white mass went. Bev then told me that when she put this particular picture on the computer screen she could see actual faces in the haze.

Suddenly the energy around Bev and me changed. Now there were three different male spirits standing right by us. One had a particularly mean scowl on his face. He started touching us and then walked through us, at which point Bev and I jumped about three feet off the ground. His energy was so cold. He came right up to my face and tried to take my breath away, which ghosts will do sometimes in order to become bigger and more powerful. Earthbound spirits can come right up to your face and take your breath as you're exhaling. It's a very suffocating feeling, like you can't get enough air. My teacher taught us to tell the spirit to back off and leave us alone when they do something like this, but you need to sound very firm.

The good news was that I could see the abusive ghost, so I told him to back off and leave us alone. I asked what his name was and what he wanted. He said his name was Raymond. He would back off for a minute or so and then come right back at both of us. He kept trying to bug us by touching us. At one point, he put one hand on my back and one hand on Bev's back at the same time, and again, she and I jumped up about three feet, yelling at him to leave us alone.

Earlier, Scott had told me that he had had to take time off from work because he had come down with chronic fatigue syndrome. I'm certain that Raymond was responsible for it, sucking Scott's energy out of him daily. He seemed like such a loser, a leech. He kept coming at me, trying to get energy from me, and at one point, I could feel myself getting drained. My teacher had told me to be very firm when dealing with ghosts like Raymond, and to tell them to back off. This was not the time to get wimpy or start believing that the ghosts had more power than me, so I told him to back off and leave me alone now! He did leave the house, but I suspected he probably came back the next day after we all left.

By this time, it was almost three-thirty in the morning. We were all getting pretty tired, so Bev brought out a bunch of food she had prepared for us. Pizza, turkey, chips—you name it, she had it. We decided to lighten up a bit and not talk about ghosts for a while, so we shut off the cameras and microphones and took a break. No sooner had I made a sandwich than one of Bev's friends, who was sitting at the top of the basement stairs, started hyperventilating, shaking, and crying. She kept saying "Get it out of me, get it out of me." It completely took me by surprise.

I looked inside of Bev's friend to see if any of the spirits had jumped into her, but saw nothing there. Bev was trying to calm her down. The producer was hollering for me to do something. The cameraman was trying to get his equipment set up to get all of this drama on film. My spirit guides were telling me to go into a room by myself because they wanted to talk to me. I yelled back to the producer that I would be there in a second, but that first I had to find out what was wrong.

The guides told me to get her into a chair in the kitchen area, because that was where the energy was positive and clear—the room where we were all laughing and not telling ghost stories! They said to burn some sage and surround her in smoke. I was to put my hand on her back and Bev's hand on her chest and instruct her to say several times, out loud: "I am clear, I am clear." Though Bev's friend was convinced that there was a spirit in her, the spirits assured me that there wasn't. They said she was very sensitive and that her body was acting like a psychic sponge, soaking up all the negative energy in the house. They said she should not be there and that as soon as we got her calmed down and cleared, we should have someone take her home.

It took a good solid five to ten minutes of reassuring her over and over that she was not filled with a negative entity, and her continually affirming out loud that she was clear— body, mind, and soul—before she finally settled down. Shaky but clearheaded, she had one of Bev's other friends drive her home. My guides had me tell her to go right to bed, not to sit up and rehash what had happened. We didn't hear from her after she left, so I assume she was okay.

By then it was close to four-thirty. We were sitting waiting for the crew to set up their equipment in Scott and

Bev's bedroom, where most of the ghost activity seemed to be. Another one of Scott's friends came over to visit and handed me a visitor's brochure about the area. He said it talked about the original settlers and a guy named Tom, who had been the sheriff back in the eigtheen hundreds. I felt shivers up my spine as I realized that this was the same Tom I had met several hours earlier.

One more room and we were done. We were all exhausted. The cameraman and audio woman were husband and wife. They were a great team, really fun to work with. They had to deal with a lot of frustration that night. First, their very expensive camera was knocked off the shelf, and all throughout the night the audio equipment had a high-pitched sound to it. The only time it would stop was when I was having a dialogue with the ghosts. We all surmised that somehow the ghosts were creating the sound and that they were quiet only when they wanted everyone to hear what they had to say.

We walked into Scott and Bev's bedroom. There, sitting in a rocking chair in the corner, was Bev's deceased grandmother. Over to the right of the chair near the closet sat Tom and his four buddies. There on Scott and Bev's bed lay two male ghosts, and there was another one standing in the corner. No wonder they felt so much activity in their bedroom. They had told me earlier about what a hard time they had sleeping in there. No kidding! This was where all the ghosts congregated. I couldn't imagine trying to get any sleep in there.

I went around to each ghost and asked it what it was doing there. Some of them wouldn't talk to me. Tom and his buddies moved in and out of the room. Grandma just liked being there. We were all so tired that I decided to just burn some sage and tell them to clear out. I was concerned about leaving some of them there, so I asked the spirits to please leave these people alone and go on to the other side. They left the building, but I don't believe they went on to the other side.

I did not do an official ghostbusting on each ghost because the producer had only wanted me to identify the ghosts, and besides, everyone just wanted to get some sleep. At about six o'clock in the morning, after heavily saging the house, we packed up our equipment and headed back to our hotel.

I have spoken with Scott and Bev a number of times since our original meeting, and they say the activity in the cabin has continued. In case you're wondering if Scott ever became a believer, he said he's going to remain on the skeptical side until he has more proof.

There's a line in the movie *The Sixth Sense* about ghosts only believing what they want to believe, and I would have to say that's just as true of many of the living. Ghosts really do exist, whether we choose to believe in them or not!

Ghost Fact

The more fuss you make about a ghost, the more ghosts you'll attract. Portals are openings from our world into the spirit world. The most common way to create one of these portals is by working the Ouija board, because it's inviting communication. The problem with opening ourselves up to the spirit world without knowing what we're doing is that we attract all kinds of souls that may not be so favorable. If you suspect you have a portal in your home, ask the universe to close it up, and read up on psychic protection. This is nothing to mess with.

THE GHOSTS
AT THE BAR

In October 1991, *Sightings* called to see if I would fly down
to Wilder, Kentucky, and check out a bar called Bobby
Mackey's Music World. The associate producer told me she
didn't want to tell me anything about this place because she
was curious to see what I would find. She said I did not have
to get rid of the ghosts, just identify them. She certainly had
my curiosity going. I figured if they were willing to fly me all
the way to Kentucky for a day, something must be up.

The day before I left, I came down with a strange cough,
and by the next day, I barely had a voice. I wasn't sure if I
should go down to Kentucky or not, but decided that once
I got there I would probably be all right. On the plane I
got concerned about how psychic I would be because my
energy was so low, so I asked God to please help me feel
more confident and give me some energy to do a good job.
I arrived in Cincinnati at about two o'clock that afternoon

and took a cab across the river to the bar in Kentucky. The cab driver asked me what I was doing in town, and with some hesitation I told him I was a psychic and was sent to this bar to see if I could find any ghosts.

I had barely spoken the whole sentence when he asked me to give him a reading on his career. I asked him what his first name was and immediately started getting psychic information on him. His career goals, relationship—it all just started flowing. Doing the reading let me know that I was on track psychically. When I arrived at the bar, the producer of the show was waiting outside for me. He quickly opened the door, helped me out of the cab, and thanked the cab driver. I looked at the driver apologetically, as if to say "Sorry I can't help you more." He was sitting there with his mouth wide open. The only thing he said was that he had never had such an experience in his life and that everything I'd said was amazingly accurate. Good, I thought. I said a quick prayer of thanks to God and moved on to the next thing, which was this bar.

The building was over one hundred years old. It was wooden, with brown paint that was chipping off everywhere. It had no windows, and it was tilting to the side. It gave off a very thick negative energy, which a lot of old bars do. There were railroad tracks in the back and a river running nearby. It was cold outside, the leaves were off the trees, and the building looked old and desolate, like it could easily fall apart in a strong wind. As I was standing there observing this scary-looking building, the producer explained to me that they wanted me to walk through by myself.

Normally when I do TV shows, the camera crew is walking about six feet ahead of me in order to catch my reactions on film. In this particular situation, they wanted me to walk through first with just a microphone on. The lighting inside was very poor, and in order to get good shots, they had to do an extensive setup for each shot.

The producer said they would give me the floor plans if that would make it easier for me. The more I looked at the place, the more creeped out I got. I finally interrupted the producer in my raspy-sounding voice and asked him if he would please walk through with me. I didn't feel that I had the energy to do it all by myself. There was something so ominous about the place, and I kept thinking that something must not be too cool in there if the TV show thought it was impressive enough to make a show out of it. Fortunately the producer said he was willing to go with me.

The crew put a microphone on me, and I began to walk through the old bar. First stop was the women's bathroom. No ghosts in there. Next was the men's room. There, standing behind one of the stalls, was a male ghost wearing cowboy boots and a cowboy hat. He startled me by smiling and saying, "Howdy, ma'am." I said howdy back and giggled as I walked out. I figured this wasn't the bad ghost I should be searching for.

We moved on to the large bar area, and there I found three male ghosts arguing at a table. I walked over to them and asked them what they were arguing about. They told me they loved to drink and get into fights. They said that they would wait until guys were drunk in the bar and then they would enter their bodies and start fights. They were very immature souls, real rowdy. Just wanted to party and fight. I kept walking. I saw a male ghost behind the bar playing bartender and a female ghost standing up on stage, singing a song. The bartender ghost told me she stood there all day, singing songs. Hmmmm. Other than the three bullies, none of these ghosts seemed to be a problem.

I told the producer I needed a couple of minutes just to get my bearings. I stood apart from everyone and psychically scanned the building. I could feel an energy down in the basement and asked the producer if we could go downstairs. The crew decided to go ahead and set up the camera equipment, so I sat for a few minutes and took a break. There were several people watching us tape. So far I had not been introduced to anyone. The producers wanted my psychic impressions first.

As soon as they had everything set up, the producter came back upstairs and got me. In order to get to the basement we had to go down a very steep set of stairs on the outside of the building. As the producer opened the door, I looked at the stairs and told myself to go slow and I would be okay. Out of the blue, something came up from behind me, put hands on my back, and pushed, *really* hard. I screamed and grabbed onto the railing. I turned around, expecting to see person standing there. Instead I saw a female ghost. I yelled at her and asked her why she had done that.

She was so shocked that I could see her that she bolted around the corner and disappeared. I asked the producer, who was now standing at the bottom of the stairs waiting for me, if one of the bad ghosts was a female who pushed people down the stairs. He told me he was impressed, but would explain more later because now we had to get to the basement while the lighting was ideal.

This basement was one of the creepiest places I had ever seen. It reeked of mold and mildew. Each room I passed seemed creepier than the last. There was junk everywhere, as if pack rats had stored things there for years and years. I could hear moaning, people talking in a different language, cows mooing, and weird chanting going on somewhere, but I couldn't find the source. Some of the rooms I just couldn't stay in. The vibes were hard to describe—they were very negative. There was such a feeling of death down there. Then I came upon a room that had two ghosts in it—a female and a male. The female was sitting down. She had her hands on her chin as if she was holding her head on her neck, and she kept saying, "Oh my head, oh my head." The male ghost was pacing back and forth and kept saying to her, "It's all your fault we're here, it's all your fault we're here."

I told the producer what I'd found, and he became very excited. He asked if there was anyone else or if I could describe the ghosts I'd seen. I could feel another male on the other side of the wall, so I walked to the next room, where I saw a male ghost about six feet tall with dark eyes, dark hair, and a thick dark mustache. He was quite agitated. I asked him if he knew the two people in the other room, and he said yes, and began pacing himself. I asked what his name was, and he said it was Scott. I walked back into the other room and asked the ghosts in there what their names were. The male said something that started with an "A," but I couldn't make it out. His eyes had a vacant stare to them and seemed so cold-blooded. The woman would not answer me. All she kept talking about was her head. That was all the information I could get from them, except that when I asked them how long they had been here, they said something about the late eighteen hundreds. I found it hard to believe that these characters might be the reason for the trip. They all seemed pretty harmless.

The producer seemed very happy with the work that I had done and told everyone to take a break and meet back upstairs in ten minutes. He wanted me to meet with the scientists they had flown in and one of the owners of the bar, Janet Mackey.

I went upstairs. My energy was getting drained by all the spirit activity. All I wanted was to get out of this damp, dark bar and breathe some fresh air. I walked over to the bar to get a drink of water, and the ghost bartender asked me if he could get me anything, which got me laughing. I told him I would get it myself, but thanks anyway. Then he disappeared. I sat there drinking my water, hoping nothing would interrupt my break. I glanced over at a folder on the bar and there was a picture of the two ghosts I had just seen down in the basement! I think I let out a yelp, I was so blown away. I had never seen actual photographs of ghosts from when they were still living. The captions identified them as Scott and Alonzo. There was also a picture of a woman named Pearl, who I realized was the woman ghost I had seen holding her head in the basement.

Amazed, I took the photos and ran over to the producer and told him that these were the three folks I'd seen down in the basement. He said it was time we all had a meeting.

I sat down with Janet Mackey, Dr Roland (not his real name), Carl (the caretaker) and the producer. I told them everything I had found. Janet explained all the things she had experienced in the bar—being pushed down the stairs when she was five and a half months pregnant and going into premature labor, seeing a headless woman walking around the bar, hearing voices telling her to get out of there, the jukebox playing the "Anniversary Waltz" when it was unplugged, employees complaining of being pushed, seeing the male bartender ghost behind the bar and a dark-haired ghost with a handlebar mustache. How eerie it was to hear her talk about some of the very things I had just seen!

Dr. Roland asked me to direct him to where I thought there was the most ghost activity. He wanted to set up his equipment there. I told him to go to the last two rooms on the right side of the basement, and he would find them there. He said he'd call up to me by walkie-talkie when he had everything ready to go. About fifteen minutes later, he called upstairs and told me that he had his instruments set up in the two rooms but that nothing was registering. He asked me to come downstairs.

I hated the thought of going back down those stairs, but I was curious to see what his equipment did. So, watching very closely for the female spirit at the stairs, I went back down. No sign of her. When I got to the rooms, I found all three ghosts right where I had last seen them. Dr. Roland had his computer set up right in the middle of the room. This computer supposedly measured ghost energy. If there was a ghost present, the bells in his computer were supposed to go off—but nothing was happening.

I asked my guides what I should do, and they told me to take the equipment and put it inside Scott's "stomach area," which would then register on the computer. I asked the doctor if it was possible for me to move his equipment, and he told me to be careful but go ahead. I walked over to Scott and asked him if he would mind if I put this gadget inside his stomach. He said he didn't mind. As soon as I did, the bells on Dr. Roland's computer went off like clockwork!

We went into the next room, where Alonzo and Pearl were, and did the same thing with them. The computer rang out with these two also, although not as strongly. I asked the doctor if we could take the computer to the female ghost at the top of the stairs, which we did, and the bells went off with her too. It was pretty exciting for me to have their presence validated.

We all went back to the bar, and Janet and Carl proceeded to tell me the story of the ghosts in Bobby Mackey's bar. It's quite a story, and it's all collected in a book by Doug Hensley called *Hell's Gate*. If this story is of interest to you, I recommend getting Doug's book. He did a ton of research on this famous bar and it's all in there.

The building was originally built in the early eighteen hundreds as a slaughterhouse. In 1802, some folks started holding satanic worship rituals there. Later on, the Cleveland mob owned and ran the building as a nightclub for many years. One of the nightclub singers, a guy named Robert Randall, got the owner's daughter, Johanna, pregnant, and the owner killed him. Johanna then poisoned her father and jumped to her death from the very steep stairs on the side of the building. Janet told me she was five and a half months pregnant at the time. The club was shut down for some time after that.

Then around 1896, either Scott Jackson or Alonzo Walling was dating a woman named Pearl Bryan. Pearl became pregnant and announced that she was going to tell the dean of the dental school, where Alonzo and Scott were students, who had gotten her pregnant if he didn't come forward and take care of her. Angered by the threat, either Alonzo or Scott chopped off Pearl's head and buried it somewhere near the bar. The two men were then hanged at the gallows in 1897, both claiming they hadn't done it—Alonzo claimed to have known about the crime but denied culpability, and threatened to haunt the bar forever after.

Patrons and employees of the bar have always said that when they smell the scent of roses in the bar they know someone is about to die. Indeed, that smell has led to a death every time. Johanna wore rose-scented perfume. I asked my guides if Johanna was the woman who tried pushing me down the stairs, and they said yes, that was her. I asked them why the three in the basement didn't go on to the other side, and they told me:

> The men were afraid if they went on to the other side, they would be sent to hell for killing Pearl.

> Pearl was still in love with Alonzo and was hoping they could work things out.

> Pearl felt her due punishment for getting pregnant was to have her head chopped off, yet she had a tremendous amount of anger towards both men and had decided to hang out and make their "lives" miserable.

Pearl could set herself free from this little triangle any-time, but so far she had chosen to stay in it. She wanted Alonzo to acknowledge his relationship to her, and until he did, she was going to stay there.

Wow. This whole thing had happened so fast, and before I knew it, it was time to leave for the airport. Once again, the media was making these ghosts out to be evil monsters, but they're not. There wasn't anything evil going on at that bar. It was just filled with a bunch of stuck souls. I didn't help get rid of them (once again, I was only hired to find them), but I was hoping they'd eventually move on.

• • •

Six years later, in June 1997, I got a phone call from a television show called *The Unexplained*. They wanted to know if I had done any really interesting stories in the last few years. I told them about Bobby Mackey's place. I had already discussed the case of several other TV programs—*The Sally Jesse Raphael Show* flew several of us to New York to talk about it on the show. *Geraldo* did a show on it, too.

The producer of *The Unexplained* called the bar to see if any more activity was going on. When they heard that it was, they called and asked me if I would be interested in doing a follow-up. I said sure. I was very curious to see if the gang was still there. I also asked the producer if we might have some extra time so that I could do a ghostbusting and send those who wanted to go to the.light. He said we would make the time.

About three weeks later, on the day I was to leave for Kentucky, I developed the strangest cough. I didn't give it much thought until the morning when I got up to go to the bar. I realized I barely had a voice. Déjà vu. This seemed pretty eerie to me. I had to take two different cabs because the drivers didn't know where I was going. I had laryngitis so bad that neither cab driver could understand me, and they didn't know where the bar was. After getting two completely different sets of directions from people on the street, we finally found the bar. I felt as if I was in the Twilight Zone.

When I walked in, I saw that nothing had changed! It was like time had stood still. Some of the same faces were still there (living people). The bar looked and smelled the same, except that this time it wasn't a fall day; it was 91 degrees outside and about one hundred degrees inside. One of the bouncers told me that a ghost had been getting into fights with people and he felt sure it was Alonzo. He also said that something or someone had hit him on the back of the head with a beer bottle, sending him to the hospital. This man is no small weakling, so it was hard to imagine.

I began my walk-through just like the last time. The women's bathroom was clear. The cowboy was no longer in the men's bathroom, but Alonzo was! I was surprised to see him upstairs. He started talking right away and asked me if I could help him get out of there. He said he hated it there. He was tired of people talking about him. He said it was like living in hell, and he had to get out of there. He couldn't take it anymore.

When I told him that I'd help him go to the other side, he wasn't sure what I was talking about. He just knew he wanted to get out of the bar. He pointed to a woman half-way down the bar and said I should talk to Johanna and see if she wanted to leave, too. When I asked him about Scott and Pearl, he didn't say much, which gave me the impression that maybe they weren't speaking to each other.

There were several male ghosts sitting up at the bar pretending that they had beer glasses in their hands and that they were drinking from them. The male bartender was still there, but his energy was very weak. I could barely see him. I approached Johanna, and right away she apologized to me for trying to push me down the stairs. I was very surprised that she remembered me, and she said that there weren't that many visitors who could actually see them, so that's why she remembered me.

She told me she was very tired of this existence and that she wanted to leave. Was there anyplace else besides this bar to live? It was as if she had been there so long, she couldn't remember any other existence. Her energy was also very weak. She didn't have the anger that she had had six years before. She was worn out. Ready to move on, I told her I was going to send Alonzo on to the other side and that she should think about whether or not she wanted to go with him. I told her I needed to continue walking through the bar and that I would be back to talk to her. She told me to watch out for Gregory, and she motioned over to the pool room. I asked her who Gregory was, and she said he was the guy that was starting all the fights. She said Alonzo wouldn't do that and that people had it all wrong. She said this Gregory was a really mean guy.

I cautiously walked over to the pool room area, where I found a male ghost standing up against the wall. He was dressed in blue jeans and a dark blue shirt. He had on cowboy boots and told me he usually wore a cowboy hat, but didn't have it on that day. I asked him if he was Gregory, and he said to call him "Buck, Buck, Buck. Call me Buck." I asked him why he was there, and he told me he was a close personal friend of Bobby Mackey's. He said he had killed a man with his bare hands. We chatted for a while. He was one angry ghost.

At one point in the conversation, Buck seemed to get tired. He told me he would be right back, and I saw him go over to the other side of the bar. I could tell he was going to suck the energy out of someone, and I thought he was headed for the bouncer, but he took energy from the female bartender instead. When I went over to the bar to see how they were feeling, she was sound asleep and the bouncer was slowly losing his energy. This Buck was not a good ghost. Another leech like Raymond.

I have very little patience for ghosts like this, so I left him and went downstairs to find Pearl and Scott. There they were, still in the last room at the end of the hall. Their energy was also very weak. I tried convincing them to go into the light with Alonzo and Johanna, but they wouldn't even consider it. They were afraid to go on to the other side, for fear of being sent to hell. I told Scott he had spent enough time in hell already just living in this basement, but he just would not budge. He and Pearl were staying. After about ten minutes I gave up and I went back upstairs.

Meanwhile, the producer had asked the bouncer to call Bobby at home and ask him if he had had any close personal friends, now deceased, named Buck. When we got back upstairs, the producer gave me four names and wanted me to tell him which Buck this was. The first name he gave me felt like the Buck that I had just spoken to, and, as it turned out, that was the Buck whose name Bobby had given them. Bobby didn't actually know if this guy was alive or dead but said that he was the black sheep of the town that he'd grown up in. He was a real mean guy who had killed his own brother, but Bobby didn't know what had ever happened to him. The producer said he'd check with the town records to see if there was a Gregory or Buck with the last name that we got, but I never heard how it all turned out. I can tell you that Alonzo and Johanna did move on into the tunnel and went over to the other side.

Here's how it happened: Before I left, I went back to the men's bathroom where Alonzo was still hanging out, and I asked him to get Johanna. Within seconds they both floated over to me, and I talked to them about moving away from this bar and looking for the tunnel. They held hands and went into the tunnel together. I told them to head right for the light, which they did. They'd both been physically dead for so long, they didn't have a lot of energy. What a relief to see them out of this bar and into the light.

Afterwards, I burned a lot of sage and walked through the entire bar, asking God to please clear out all of the negative vibes in there. I warned the bouncer not to let Buck steal his energy and told him that it was important that he ask God for protection, because he seemed so vulnerable to these spirits.

All in all, it was a pretty successful trip. I had a terrible case of laryngitis that lasted for almost a week after I got back, but it was well worth it for me to see those two ghosts from the eighteen hundreds get free.

Ghost Fact

Ghosts and spirits have no concept of time. They can remain in the same room or area for years and years, never giving any thought to how long they've been dead or how much life is changing around them. They are literally stuck at a point in time in their consciousness. Honesty is the best way to handle a situation like this. We tell the ghost, "This is the year 2000; it's important for you to move into the light."

THE GHOST WHO
KEPT ENTERING
HIS BODY

Every year around Halloween, Michael and I would hear
from someone in the media who wanted to do a piece on
ghosts. One year, the television show *Encounters* called and
asked if we had any interesting ghost stories. I told them
we didn't have anything right then but that I'd call as soon
as I got something. It's always so amazing to me how these
so-called coincidences work. By the end of the day, we got
a call from a woman who thought she had ghosts.

She said she was very frightened to stay in her home and
could feel something watching her. She was afraid to go
down to the basement because three cats had mysteriously
died down there. She and her boyfriend—I will call them
Kelly and Dick—heard banging on the walls and windows.
Doors would open on their own. When they lay in bed at

night they could hear music coming up the vents. Kelly told us that Dick's behavior would get really strange from time to time. Although he was normally a very mild-mannered, almost timid man, one time he tried to strangle her in the middle of the night. Other times he would kick and scream at her. She said one time she found him unconscious at the bottom of the stairs. An ambulance took him to the hospital, and the hospital put him in restraints because he had gone berserk. When Dick woke up, he had no recollection of the events that had taken place.

I called the show, and they were very interested in doing a story on this.

When Michael and I got to Kelly and Dick's house, we walked through it and found the ghost, Joe, right away. What an angry ghost he was. We first discovered him in the bedroom. The camera crew got all set up. We were prepared to talk to Joe and find out what his story was, but as soon as we were ready to talk to him, he disappeared down through the floor to the laundry room, the room Kelly hated to go into.

Michael ran downstairs to talk to him. The camera crew went down with him. Once again, as soon as everything was set up to begin shooting, Joe disappeared up through the floor, and there I was, face to face with a very angry ghost. Fortunately the camera crew had walkie-talkies, so Michael and I used those to talk to each other. This ghost was all over the place. He did not want to be pinned down or talked to.

Dick became very uptight with all the activity in the house. He told us he needed to sit outside and get away from the crowd. At first it didn't seem odd, because Dick was very shy and it just seemed reasonable that he would want to be off by himself. The problem, though, was that as soon as Dick went outside, we could not find Joe anywhere. It was just so eerie. Paul Johnson, the forensic sketch artist, sat Michael and me down at the kitchen table to make a composite sketch of Joe. He had each of us pick out Joe's features—eyebrows, eyes, nose, cheeks, lips, nose, chin, ears, and hair—from several cards he had with him. We both picked out the exact same feature each time. We'd never done this before, so it was kind of fun for us to know that we really do see the same things.

After we were done with the sketch, we continued to walk through the house looking for Joe, but were having no luck at all. The producer was getting impatient and told us to make Joe come out now, because we had to get the show on the road. We realized that the producer had no concept of what was going on here. He wanted to get the show in the can, as they say, but you can't *make* a ghost do anything. We explained to him that Joe had disappeared and it was just a matter of waiting because we knew he would be back. Suddenly it dawned on me that maybe, just maybe, Joe had gone inside of Dick. I called to my brother, who had gone downstairs to look for Joe, on the walkie-talkie and asked him what he thought of the idea, and he called back to say his guides agreed that that was exactly what had happened. Joe had gone into Dick, as he had done on several occasions. That was why Dick couldn't be around any of us—because we would've been able to see Joe in Dick's eyes.

Michael's guides went on to say that years ago this fellow, Joe, had accidentally overdosed on drugs, trying to get his girlfriend's attention. He told her he was going to kill himself, she called his bluff, and he accidentally overdosed. The guides said Kelly reminded Joe of his old girlfriend, and that is why he tried to strangle her when he was inside Dick's body. We asked how he came to this house, and they said he used to buy his drugs from one of the former owners of the house before Kelly bought it. What a story!

We explained all of this to the producer and he really perked up. He wanted the crew to set up the lighting and their cameras before I told Dick what was going on, because they wanted to get his reaction on camera. I felt bad for Dick. I wouldn't want someone explaining something like that to me with a bunch of cameras in my face. As soon as everything was set up, the producer went outside and asked Dick to come into the house. Dick was reluctant to come in. He sat staring at us for a few seconds, almost as if he was trying to figure out how to get out of there. I think it was actually Joe who was hesitating, because he knew what we knew. Dick finally did come into the kitchen and I explained to him that Joe was inside of him, possessing his body, and that we wanted to channel a healing to him and pull Joe out of him. Dick was very willing to do whatever he had to in order to get rid of this spirit once and for all.

Michael stood behind Dick, put his hands on his shoulders, and began channeling healing energy to him. I stood in front of Dick and started pulling Joe out of Dick's chest. Dick could feel the entity coming out. Dick was moaning and his body was jerking as I pulled Joe's soul out. They got it all on camera.

As soon as Joe was out of Dick, I continued to channel a healing to him, while Michael talked with Joe about the importance of getting on with his life by going to the other side. After about twenty minutes, Joe did go. I continued to fill Dick's body up with healing energy while Michael saged the entire house. We had Kelly walk through the house, and she said it felt completely different.

Three weeks later, Kelly called to say Joe was back. Something felt very odd about the whole thing, and I couldn't put my finger on it. I asked my guides what to do, and they said this time it was up to Dick to stand up to Joe and tell him to get out of his body. They said that Joe had entered Dick again because Dick had a problem with recognizing his own power. He saw Joe as more powerful than himself, and this was one of Dick's life lessons. He had to start standing up for himself. They said that if he didn't stand up to Joe, he would continue to be plagued by his presence or other spirits like him.

When I explained to Dick how to do this, what he needed to say and all, he was quite hesitant about the whole thing. He said a couple of times that he didn't think he could do it. My guides told me again that it was important that Dick do this, not me or Michael. We didn't hear from them again, but some mutual friends told me that Kelly and Dick split up. Dick moved out, and Kelly had a new boyfriend. I hope for Dick's sake that he stood up to Joe and set both men free.

Ghost Fact

Ghosts can be very self-serving. They do what they want without considering what it's doing to others. Don't ever let a ghost "have its way with you," no matter what that means. If you suspect that you're being taken over by a ghost, do not under any circumstances put up with it. Ghosts need to honor boundaries just like the rest of us!

THE GHOSTS
WHO WERE
PEEPING TOMS

I pause as I think about writing this chapter on peeping tom ghosts simply because I hate to plant the seed that there are these types of ghosts out there. But truth be told, there are.

A couple of such experiences come to mind that I'd like to share with you. The first one took place at the beautiful Heathman Hotel in Portland, Oregon. Whenever I've gone to Portland to do a book signing, my publisher always puts me up in the Heathman. On this particular trip to Portland, I was promoting my fourth book, *Relax, It's Only a Ghost,* and the Heathman happened to have a haunted room. Room 703. They gave me that room as well as a room that was not rumored to be inhabited by a ghost.

I dropped off my luggage at the (supposedly) uninhabited room first and headed down to room 703 to see what

I could find. When I walked in, the radio, television, and radio were all on, so I called down to the front desk to see if they had left them on for me. The person at the desk assured me that no appliance had been left on when housekeeping was finished with the room. I looked around to see if there were any ghosts in the room, but I saw nothing, so I went back to my ghost-free room.

I'm a multi-tasker, so while unpacking, getting ready to take a shower, and ironing all at the same time, I started to feel eyes peering at me. At first I thought it was my imagination. This room was supposedly ghost-free, so I just kept doing what I was doing. I turned on the TV and started running the water for my shower when the feelings of someone watching me became more noticeable. As much as I did not want to open up psychically and see someone standing there; I figured I better get to the bottom of the feelings because I was feeling less and less like taking a shower.

I opened up my third eye and there stood a male ghost with this creepy look on his face. I asked him what he was doing there and he said, "Watching you."

I asked the ghost if he was the ghost from room 703. He laughed and said that that's what they call him, but that he roams all over the hotel. I asked him why he was staying earthbound and he told me that he liked watching the women. This ghost absolutely creeped me out, so I told him to get out of my room. He did leave right away which was great, but later that night, when I was reading in bed, I could feel him standing over in the corner watching me. I put my book down, stared right at him, and told him to get the hell out of my room, which he did. Then I asked my spirit guide to seal the room up in white light so that he would leave me alone for the rest of the night. I had a peaceful night's sleep.

The next day, as I was wheeling my suitcase to the front desk to check out, I saw the lascivious ghost in the hallway, floating into someone else's room. He obviously wanted to stay, and the hotel didn't ask me to get rid of him, so I didn't try talking him into the light.

• • •

Another related story comes to mind. Three deceased motorcycle riders were hanging out in the bedroom closet of a young couple's trailer. I was called to this home because, according to the woman, something was pulling her three-year-old son down the hallway. I had never heard of such a thing and was very curious to see how a ghost would be able to pull this off.

As I walked through the trailer, I could feel this really creepy voyeuristic energy coming from the room in the back. As I walked by the bathroom, I could see an energy that moved back and forth through the walls, spending some of the time in the bathroom and the rest of the time in the bedroom closet. I hated going into that room because it felt so gross to me—like a slimy peeping tom was lurking behind the closet doors.

I could hear some laughter and mumbling, but the voices and energy were quite blurry. As I got closer to the closet, I saw three male earthbound spirits just standing there with grins on their faces—like they had been caught. Two of the men were not very scary. They seemed to just be tagging along with this other male ghost who was defintely the peeping tom of the bunch. I asked what they were doing there, and the main guy told me that they had all been killed in motorcycle accidents and chose to hang out in the trailer because of the couples' love for motorcycles and because this young woman was *hot*.

The ghosts loved watching her in the shower and getting dressed, they told me. All I wanted to do was get the heck out of there, but I felt a strong desire to get them out of her house first. I asked if any of them was responsible for dragging the three-year-old down the hall. The ghosts all laughed, but no one took responsibility for it (to this day I don't know how they could do something like that).

It took almost an hour of talking to these guys to convince them to move on to the other side. They all thought heaven was going to be a very strict, formal type of atmosphere, and they just wanted to party with other bikers and have a good time. What finally got them to go was when I reassured them that heaven is not a stuffy place but similar to earth in many ways—and that there were lots of bikers on the other side, still having a good time.

I checked with the young woman a few days later to make sure everything was back to normal, and she said that for the first time since moving in, she no longer felt creepy when she took a shower or got undressed in her bedroom.

You might be wondering if all ghosts who inhabit bathrooms are peeping toms, and I can assure you that most are not. I've met at least a dozen ghosts who hang out in people's bathrooms simply because it's a nice quiet room in the house—they could care less if the person is taking a shower.

Ghost Fact

If you do sense that someone is watching you when you're in your bathroom, just tell them to leave. Or better yet, instead of waiting to feel like someone is watching you, ask your spirit guides to clear out any peeping toms who are lurking in your home. That should do the trick.

THE GHOST WHO LIKED SEX

A woman named Sandy called several times regarding a ghost problem she was having. Every time I talked to her, I had a strange feeling about her and her situation, but I could never put my finger on what it was. My intuition told me not to waste my time going out to her house because it wouldn't solve the problem, but of course I felt compelled to do what I could for her. I asked my assistant, who had done many ghost jobs with me, if she would go and check the place out.

My assistant went to Sandy's house and found a male ghost who she convinced to leave, but she called me to say that she felt he would probably be back. She said she could sense a strong connection between Sandy and her ghost, but she didn't know what it was. About two weeks later, Sandy called to say her ghost was back. She wanted my assistant to return and fix the problem, which she did—two more times.

But it didn't end there. My brother, Michael, went to Sandy's house on another occasion, as did one of my advanced students who had taken over the ghostbusting part of my business. In every case, they thought they had gotten the ghost to move on, but he would always come back.

Several years after all this started, Sandy called me for a psychic reading. She told me that her ghost was still there and was now doing terrible, nasty things to her. She said she had spent all kinds of money trying to get rid of him, but to no avail. I had a strong intuitive feeling that the timing was right this time and that I would finally be able to figure out what this was all about, so I agreed to do the reading.

The first image that came to me was of Sandy's most recent past life. I could see that she'd been married to the man who was now haunting her home. My guides said this male spirit was very possessive of her and that her soul was also possessive of him. They said that this couple had been—and obviously continued to be—literally addicted to each other, and that their souls had hoped that by coming back to earth at different times they would break their addiction. But that's not how it was turning out. His ghost found her and they are continuing their addictive relationship.

The guides said the only way Sandy could get rid of this ghost was by standing up to him and telling him to leave her alone. They also said they seriously doubted she would do this because she obviously liked having him there. As far as the "nasty things" went, my guides said that the ghost was being sexual with her, but that she was consenting to it. As you can tell, my guides weren't particularly sympathetic. They could see that she was choosing to be "victimized" by this male spirit and that nothing would work until she was really ready to give him up.

Ghost Fact

This might be more human fact than ghost fact. If you are getting a lot of attention, whether it's negative or positive, from having a ghost in your house and there's some kind of pay-off in it for you, it's YOU that's keeping the ghost there.

The Ghost Who Pushed Her Out of Bed

It always boggles my mind when we get a call about a ghost physically assaulting someone. It's hard for me to wrap my head around the idea that a ghost made of nothing but energy can actually harm a physical being.

In my experience with physically abusive ghosts, the ghost is usually filled with deep emotion (rage, guilt, shame, hatred). Strong emotion generates the kind of energy that is powerful enough to physically harm a human being. In this particular case, the ghost was filled with jealousy.

Sherrie was a female ghost who had been murdered by her boyfriend who then committed suicide. Sherrie didn't want to go anywhere near her ex, so she decided to hang out on the earth plane and find herself a new boyfriend.

Enter the homeowner Jake, a very handsome young man in his early thirties who was engaged to be married. Sherrie latched onto unsuspecting Jake, and problems began to occur whenever his fiancée would spend the night.

Sherrie became very jealous of Jake's fiancée and would frequently push her out of bed when she spent the night. Jake's fiancée thought he was the one pushing her out of the bed, and they had several arguments around it. Other strange events were taking place whenever she was there: lights turning on and off, the TV turning off by itself. Jake's fiancée kept feeling a cold presence move through her as if to get her to leave. When she put her foot down and told Jake she wouldn't be coming back until the problem was solved, he called me out of desperation.

Sherrie was not shy about introducing herself. She was quite anxious for me to understand what was going on in Jake's house. She told me that Jake was HER boyfriend and that she loved him and loved making love to him at night. She was sure that Jake was in love with her too, and said she had to get rid of the fiancée so she could have him all to herself.

I stood watching this very confident spirit and wondered how in the world I was going to get her to move on to the other side. I also wondered how much I should say to Jake about her "making love" comment. I didn't know this man, and I wasn't sure how he'd take the news that a ghost was having sexual relations with him at night. But if this was something he was experiencing, it would be very helpful for him to understand it.

I told Jake everything that Sherrie had said. He didn't seem all that surprised, but he insisted that he didn't know anyone named Sherrie who was deceased. He did confirm that he had dreams of a female stranger making love to him at night. He said it felt more real than just a dream, but couldn't imagine it being anything other than a very vivid dream.

My guides told me that the only way we were going to get Sherrie to move on was to have Jake be the one to tell her to leave. He had to be very firm with her, because she wasn't about to leave him on her own. I showed him where she was standing and told him to treat her like an intruder in his house. I instructed him to tell her that she had to leave and go to the other side. He told her several times that she had to leave and never come back; after hearing this enough and seeing that he was serious, Sherrie finally did leave.

I talked to Jake about a month after the ghostbusting job and he assured me that everything was back to normal. He and his fiancée were happily planning their upcoming wedding.

THE GHOST WHO TRIED TO STRANGLE ME

I told you in the last chapter that when I hear stories of ghosts who have tried to hurt people, my analytical Virgo mind has a tough time understanding how they can actually do it.

This is one of those rare stories of me being assaulted by a ghost. They don't happen often, but they do crop up every once in a while. I was on the West Coast shooting a piece for a television show. It was Halloween, and the show was sponsoring a contest for the most haunted house in Seattle. Many people sent in their stories, but this one particular story was of special interest to the producers.

As always, I had no idea what I was walking into as I strolled through a very old, large Seattle mansion. The house felt lonely. Most of the rooms were empty. As I came walking up the stairs to the second floor, I could feel an energy focused on me, but I couldn't see any ghosts. I went into one of the bedrooms and encountered some very strange energy—it was creepy and very hard to describe. Several of the smaller rooms had the same bizarre energy, and I felt like I didn't want to spend any more time in them than I absolutely had to.

I came around a corner and out of the blue, a very angry Spanish female ghost wrapped her hands around my neck and squeezed as tight as she could. My body slammed back against the wall as I tried to make sense of what was happening. The ghost was screaming at me in Spanish, which I didn't understand. My guide told me that this ghost was very jealous of any woman who entered the house because the homeowner was her boyfriend/lover. She wanted me out of there. I literally needed to step way back to get the ghost-woman's energy off of me, and I yelled at her to leave me alone.

She had long, straggly black hair, olive skin, and jet-black eyes. She was disheveled in old, messy, off-the-shoulder clothes. She appeared worn out and desperate.

I asked the renter if he was aware of a jealous female ghost. He laughed and said that he was very aware of her—that she tried to strangle every woman who came into the house, and that he thought it was kind of cute, even though it wreaked havoc on his love life.

When I asked the ghost, she told me that they had a great sex life, that she completely satisfied him, and that he didn't need any other women. I was dumbfounded; I didn't know what to say. The man stood there with this smile on his face that made my skin crawl. Maybe this explained those indescribable vibes in that bedroom. I didn't know and I didn't want to know—I just wanted to get out of that house and not ever go back. I didn't share the information with the man because I felt so creeped out, but I did share it with the producer of the show as we drove away from the house. That's when the producer confirmed that the reason we had gone to this man's house in the first place was because he had told her he was having a sexual relationship with a ghost

Ghost Fact

Ghosts are able to physically harm us by taking energy either from us or from someone in the room. If you are being attacked by a ghost, DEMAND that they leave you alone and GET OUT OF YOUR HOUSE. You are the one with the power. Don't ever forget that.

The Ghosts Who Were Controlling Their Lives

As soon as I walked into the Long Island home, I could see trouble sitting on a chair in the living room. His energy was so hateful—so angry and resentful that this family was living in "his home." I had to step back outside and get my bearings after feeling all the negative energy coming from this ghost. I walked around on the grass to get grounded until the director called me back into the house to begin filming a ghost job for a possible TV show.

I walked past the angry ghost in the living room and headed for the bedrooms. There was a little girl ghost hiding under the desk in one of the teenage daughters' bedrooms; and the ghost's deceased mother was hiding in the closet. The little girl was just a delight, but the mother was filled with shame for killing the two of them in a car accident when she was intoxicated. Her aura was very gray and filled with heavy emotion.

The next room I walked into had the soul of a sixteen-year-old girl sitting on the bed. She showed me her "arms," which were covered with tattoos, and told me that she would convince whoever that slept in that room to get a tattoo like hers. I asked her how she had died, and she said in a motorcycle accident. She seemed so lost and fixated on her tattoos, like they were the only things in the world she cared about.

The next ghost who appeared to me was Tom, the male ghost in the bathroom. He was quite outgoing and kept walking through me to get a rise out of me. I asked one of the crew members to feel Tom's energy, and he could feel Tom put a hand on his back and the cold energy move through his body.

The master bedroom was a bit creepier than Tom in the bathroom. There were five entities reclined on the bed; they all looked dazed and confused. They were acting very odd, talking but not making any sense. My guides told me that these five entities negatively affected the dreams of the husband and wife while they slept. She doubted that either of them had had a good night's sleep in at least five years. She also doubted that either of the humans ever woke up clear-headed. I didn't want to walk into the room once I saw the ghosts—it was the creepiest feeling. Totally yucky.

The next room was the biggest surprise to me. It was the bedroom of the seventeen-year-old daughter, who had left to go to a party. By some of the behavior I observed in her, I suspected that her room would be very haunted— but there was no ghost in there. I stood there in disbelief until my guide told me that the young girl actually had three entities attached to her that were always trying to get her to go out and have a good time. "Party hard. Be wild and crazy." The girl acted as a host to the three entities, and she did exactly as they wanted her to do. That these entities thought this was acceptable behavior was very upsetting to me.

While the camera crew was interviewing one of the paranormal investigators, I sat down with the mother (the owner of the house) and told her everything I had found. She was not surprised by any of it.

She told me she had not slept well or had any nice dreams in at least five years and that she always woke up in a state of confusion. She verified that her family would hear little footsteps running down the hall and see a wispy gray energy go chasing after it. She wasn't surprised to hear about Tom in the bathroom. She said that many times while she was sitting on the commode, she saw a door leading into the master bedroom—which was hard to open by itself—open and close repeatedly as if someone was standing in the doorway letting her know he was there.

She also confirmed that the daughter who slept in the bedroom where the young tattooed ghost was had indeed gotten a tattoo on her neck when she turned sixteen.

But the biggest challenge of the evening was the old man ghost sitting in the living room chair. He really did believe that he belonged there and the family didn't. He wanted them out, along with the dogs and cats. He couldn't stand the constant bickering between the two daughters; he wanted silence.

What was most upsetting was how the ghosts' negative energy was affecting the family. When anyone sat in the living room, they would start to feel angry and argumentative. The ghost would constantly tell the family to get out and leave him alone. His anger fueled disagreements among family members. He was constantly creating chaos simply by sitting in the chair with all of his anger and hatred—and the family would react to it negatively without realizing what was going on. Needless to say, it was a mess.

Tom, the ghost in the bathroom, seemed to be the most clear-headed of all of them, so I asked him to help me get everyone into the light. Between the two of us, we convinced each ghost to come into the livingroom. Then I asked Tom to lead the way to the other side. I talked to the ghosts as they made their way through the tunnel and saw the whole gang go into the light.

Unfortunately, the teenage daughter was at a party and I wasn't able to talk to her directly about the entities she was carrying around, so I wrote her a note of instruction telling her to demand that they get off of her. As I was writing the note, I saw a picture of her at a friend's house. She had her back to me so I couldn't see what she was doing, but it looked like ever since the night when she got stoned at a friend's party, these entities had been attached to her.

I told her mother about the vision. She said that her daughter had been to a friend's house about two years prior. They had been playing with the Ouija board against the mom's advice. She said that when her daughter came home the next day, she was *different*—and hadn't been her old self since then.

I asked a member of the crew to open a window in each room as I walked around with holy wood from Peru, cleansing and clearing each room of the negative energies from the ghosts. When I left, the house felt entirely different—the mom agreed.

Ghost Fact

Ghost attachment is becoming more well-known by paranormal investigators, but be aware that many of them are calling every problem on the planet ghost attachment. If a ghost has attached itself to you, it is because you need to learn to set boundaries with these entities. The main symptoms of spirit attachment are personality changes and lethargy. If you suspect that you have a spirit attachment, DEMAND that they get off of you and leave you alone.

CHILDREN WHO CAN SEE GHOSTS

My three-year-old granddaughter recently asked her daddy if she could sleep in her parents' room because there was a "lady" in her room. I asked him if she displayed any other characteristics of seeing spirits, and he mentioned that she has invisible friends that she plays with. He wasn't sure what to make of it—how would she know to fictionalize a story about a "lady" in her room or about her invisible friends?

It is not uncommon for children to see ghosts, spirits, deceased loved ones, and deceased animal spirits. The stories we hear from parents and the children themselves are not figments of their imaginations. Children really do see these entities; they haven't yet been taught that these things don't exist. In their little worlds, ghosts and spirits are as real as we are.

Many of the ghostbustings that Michael and I have been on started when children complained to their parents about "people in their rooms" or "mean people in the basement." The parents thought the kids were making these things up until the noises and strange activity got out of hand. That's when we'd get called in.

In one instance, the two children were terrified to sleep in their bedroom. They were afraid of "the mean man and woman" who they said lived in their room. I remember walking into the kids' bedroom and finding a very crabby-looking man and woman who said that they needed to be there to keep the children in line. They were the sweetest little kids. It didn't seem to me that they needed scolding from two dead people.

Another home that we were called to had a "nanny ghost" who sang opera every night when the family ate dinner. That wasn't the issue so much as the problems that the teenager of the family was having with the cranky ghost. It really irritated the ghost when the teenager and her mom would have an argument, so the "nanny ghost" would pull the teenager's hair when she was upset with her. It got to the point where the teen didn't want to come home unless someone was there with her.

And then there was the job with the little girl who was terrified to sleep in her room and kept complaining to her mom that people were sleeping in her bed. The mom thought that her little girl was making up these stories in order to sleep in bed with her, but when the girl seemed beside herself with fright, the mother called us in. We discovered six ghosts on the girl's bed. They seemed very confused about their existence and thought they were still at the mental institution where they had lived for years. When we shared the story with the mom, she confirmed that her house was built on ground that had once held an insane asylum. She said it had been torn down years before, so obviously the ghosts had remained there since they died.

One of the creepier stories in my memory bank is of the clowns. A little girl had a room full of clown dolls and complained to her mom that they would move around at night. The mom thought this was just her daughter's overactive imagination and didn't think much of it. One night, however, she slept in the girl's room to prove to her that everything was okay. Once the lights went out, the clowns slowly started moving around. The mom called us the next day, and we found several ghosts on the young girl's bed, fascinated with all the clowns.

A very sweet story comes to mind of a haunted vintage shop here in the Twin Cities called The Cottage House. Ted, the owner, asked us to come and check the place out because of some strange happenings late at night when he was there working by himself. He didn't tell us what was going on until after we did our walk-through. It was a pretty typical scenario: three male ghosts in one bedroom, just hanging out because they loved the vintage stuff. A female ghost who had drowned in the tub would roam the halls, making herself somewhat visible, so that Ted would have conversations with her, thinking that she was one of the vendors. But the ghost who I really liked was little Elizabeth. There is a unique kind of cubby hole in April's room (each vendor has their own room) and this little ghost lived in there. She played with the toys and told me she really liked the shoes April bought because they had pretty bows on them—she thought they were just for her. She told me that her mom always told her not to go down the stairs by herself, which helped Ted understand why he always heard a little girl crying at the top of the stairs.

When I asked her why she didn't want to go into the light, she said she wanted to stay there with Ted because she really liked him. When I relayed the story to Ted, he told me that one of the former vendors had a five-year-old daughter who used to come to the Cottage with her mom. She would always go upstairs to April's room and play in the cubby hole for hours with her imaginary friend.

Ghost Fact

If your child is telling you about an imaginery friend or complaining that there is a ghost in her bedroom, listen to her. Ask simple questions. Ask them to show you where the ghost is. Go over to the area and tell the ghost to move on to the light. If it's an imaginary friend, it's probably their spirit guide—and you don't need to worry about them.

FAMOUS GHOSTS

One area that people always want to know about is famous dead people. The number one question I hear is whether or not I've seen Elvis.

Fortunately for me, I'm able to tune in to the other side when someone passes over and I can see how they're doing within the first twenty-four hours after they passed. After their funerals, there's a period of time when they are not available to view, and it's because they too are going through a grieving process.

One recent Hollywood death was that of pop icon Michael Jackson. He made his transition to the other side very quickly, and came back to visit his family right away. I was surprised at his clarity. He was completely conscious of what had happened, and his soul was ready to be on the other side. During the first week of his death, I saw him very busy on this side, watching over his children and family members. He was trying so hard to get their attention, to let them know that he was going to be fine. At one point, I had a vision of him on the other side talking to Elvis Presley. It was an outdoor scene. There was a stream of water and they were sitting on the bank, talking about Lisa Marie and life in general. It seemed so peaceful; they were both talking nonstop.

There were so many people who Michael was looking forward to seeing and meeting.

Farrah Fawcett was another famous person who we lost on the very same day as Michael Jackson. My vision of her was very different. I saw her on the other side, surrounded by all the women in her family—mother, aunts, grandmothers. It was the sweetest picture of them surrounding her in white light of love and protection because she was so fragile. She remained on the other side, but did attend her funeral, which she went to with an entourage of protectors from the other side.

David Carradine was a different story. He died right around the same time as these other two stars, but his transition took a bit longer. He had died of aspyhixiation in a closet, and when I checked in on his soul, he was very confused about what had happened. For three days he thought he was dreaming. At the end of the third day, I saw one of his guides finally convince him that his life had ended. He was not happy about it.

Carradine was in a fog for several days after his death. It took a while, but eventually he started working at being at peace with his death.

Brittany Murphy, a beautiful young actress who died from pnuemonia at the age of thirty-two, was fairly surprised to find herself on the other side. I saw a *nana* there who was tending to her. As her head cleared out and she became more conscious of where she was, she really tried getting in contact with her husband and mother to say that she was sorry for leaving them. I've seen that many times in readings from the deceased—a sincere apology that they left their loved ones behind.

John F. Kennedy, Jr. went straight on to other side. I saw his mother and father waiting for him in the tunnel because they knew his plane was going down and that he was going to die that day. His wife Caroline wanted to reach her parents first to let them know that she was okay before she went on to the other side, and I saw her here on this side for several days after her death. There were many people she wanted to contact before settling in on the other side.

Princess Diana remained on this side during the entire first week of her death because she was so concerned about her sons. She had people from the other side here with her to help protect her and give her strength over the week leading up to her funeral. She did attend her funeral, but was surrounded by her family from the other side. She sat right with the boys. As she looked around, she could barely comprehend that this enormous display of affection was for her. My guides told me a few months later when I checked in to see how she was doing that she did review her funeral again when she was more clear-headed. And when Mother Theresa passed over, Princess Diana was one of the first people to greet her.

There were so many people passing over to the other side in the last few years—I can't write about them all. But of all the famous people who have died and remained earthbound for quite some time, John Belushi stayed the longest. He was so upset that he had died. When I saw him, he kept yelling, "I've been ripped off, I've been ripped off. I shouldn't be here. I've been ripped off."

When I made the suggestion to him that he move on to the other side, he just kept yelling the same thing over and over. It felt like he was trying to get some justice for his death. He has since moved on and is doing just fine on the other side.

This next story is more of a fun famous spirit story than a ghost story. It happened back in the early 90s. A woman came to me for a psychic reading. One of her questions was that she wanted to know if my guides agreed with several psychics who all told her that she was a certain person in her very recent past life. She told me nothing more, so I waited for my guides to respond to her question.

Within a minute, the soul of Elvis Presley came into my office and said "Hi, Mare." I'm sure my mouth was hanging wide open as I sat there staring at the *King*. He began a dialogue with her (me translating what he was saying) and everything indicated that they had been very close friends. He looked wonderful—young, healthy, vibrant, and quite happy to see her and talk to her again.

After Elvis was finished speaking to her, the soul of John F. Kennedy came into my office. Now, even I was questioning my sanity. He too said the name "Mare" and said it was great to see her again. This was followed by a visit from Peter Lawford, who called the woman Marilyn. They all stood talking to their old friend Marilyn Monroe, reminiscing about the good ol' days. They were all so gracious, so gentle with her. It was really fun to be a part of that experience.

After the spirits left, I asked the woman if it was true that other psychics had told her she was Marilyn Monroe in a past life. She said that every one of them had told her that, and that this wasn't the first time Elvis Presley or JFK had showed up to one of her sessions.

Ghost Fact

People have a tendency to pull on the soul of a deceased person when they die. That can be tough on the soul. When you hear of someone dying, always encourage them to go into the light instead of staying here and remaining earthbound. You don't want to encourage anyone to become a ghost. It's not good karma!

WHAT TO DO WHEN YOU GO TOO FAR

Shortly after my mom and I were told that we had psychic abilities, our lives changed. We became obsessed with spirits, ghosts, and life beyond this earthly plane.

I was so curious about my deceased loved ones and spirit guides and was constantly looking for a sign of their presence. If a light bulb flickered or the house creaked, I wondered if they were trying to contact me. If anything in my room was out of place, I figured they had moved it to get my attention. I remember spending many slumber parties with my girlfriends, us all scared out of our wits at the thought that spirits were trying to communicate with us.

I can also remember feeling a negative presence in my room and other parts of the house, sensing someone watching me, and hiding under my covers at night for fear of seeing something. I saw a head floating in the hallway one night and another time a man, though only from the waist up, standing at the end of my bed.

Sometimes I would feel a cold energy move through my body. Candles would blow out all by themselves. I would hear mumbling voices but could never make out any specific words. Sometimes the spirits would move the needle on my record player (some of you probably don't even know what that is!) or they'd change the channel on the television set (this was before the invention of the remote control). Flickering lights, heads walking down the hall, mumbling voices—no wonder I was half scared out of my wits and slept with the lights on every night.

To make matters worse, against the advice of our psychic teacher, Birdie, my mom and I decided to buy an Ouija board. Bringing that board into the house was one of the stupidest things we've ever done. Talk about opening up to the spirit world! It was insanity. But we loved to ask questions and watch that little "thingy" (the planchette) move around the board and spell out messages. We would consult that board on a daily basis.

Birdie had warned us not to play with it until we were better at seeing spirits and could determine who we were communicating with, but *not* knowing made it even more exciting. To be perfectly honest, we were drama junkies. We loved to be scared and excited, and the board provided all that and more.

After a while, though, the board started spelling out really negative, menacing messages. It would tell us that we were going to be killed in car accidents or get really sick and die—things like that. We had opened ourselves up to the fun and excitement of communicating with spirits, but the spirits we were attracting were far from positive. They would tell us they were high spiritual beings and that they worked for God, but their messages were getting more and more negative and we eventually had to get rid of the board.

I'll never forget the night we finally decided we'd had enough. The family was sitting around the dinner table and we could hear voices calling my name in a sickly tone of voice. "Echo, Echo, come here. Echo, Echo, come here." We were pretty scared. My mom called Birdie and she said that the voices were coming from the spirits attracted to the Ouija board and that they wanted us to play the board because they had a message for us. She told mom to burn the board in the fireplace and never to play with another one again. We were so addicted to it that the thought of burning it seemed cruel, so mom took it out to the garbage. The next morning when we came down to breakfast, the board was sitting on the kitchen table! Needless to say, we burned it that day.

Looking back on all the scary experiences we had with that board, I understand what my teacher meant when she said to stay away from Ouija boards until we knew what we were doing. Here's my advice to any of you out there who think it would be fun to mess around with the Ouija board: until you've worked at developing your psychic abilities and can see or hear them, I suggest you NOT get involved in all of this. You don't know what or who you could be calling into your life. I liken it to fixing a car without ever learning about car engines. Or performing surgery on someone when you've never been to medical school. You want to have a lot of knowledge before opening yourself up to the paranormal world. Read books by respected authors. Attend lectures by well-reputed psychics and spiritual teachers. Focus on the positive rather than the negative. There are plenty of books written about demons and devils if you want to get scared, but why do that to yourself? The thoughts you send out are what you will attract back to you, so focus on the good rather than the negative. Be smart.

SIGNS THAT YOU HAVE A GHOST

You might be wondering how you can tell if you have a ghost. First, you should know that there's rarely just one ghost in a house; if there's one ghost, you can bet there are more. One reason for this is that ghosts will look for a house that already has some earthbound spirits in it, so that they don't feel so alone. But though they may choose a house to live in that has other ghosts, they don't necessarily hang out with each other. They are always aware of each other; that doesn't mean they "socialize." If they weren't much on socializing when living in a body, they often just continue on that way in death. We have, on occasion, found a home that has only one ghost, and that ghost usually wants to be left alone.

Listed on the following pages are the most common signs that you've got a ghost.

- Tapping or knocking on the walls

- Doorbell ringing when no one is there

- Radio and/or television going on and off by itself

- Sounds of footsteps

- Sounds of breathing

- Water faucets being turned on by themselves

- Music playing with no obvious source

- Books or other objects being knocked off shelves

- Clothes thrown out of closets

- Wastepaper baskets turned upside down

- Burners turned on on the stove

- A cold spot in the room and no draft or window nearby

- Material possessions moved from room to room

- A white or grayish hazy object floating through a room

- Something touches you but no one is there

- A feeling of someone sitting down on your couch or bed

- Children claiming they can see someone that you can't

- Something pulling your hair or tugging on your clothes

- Your house has been for sale for a long time and no one will buy it

This last symptom is an interesting one. Over the years we have been called by several realtors who have done everything they could to sell a home, but with no success. In each case, when we came to check things out we found a ghost living in the home, and the ghost did not want anyone buying the house. In one situation, the original builder of the house had died and didn't want any new people moving in. He liked the current tenants. In another situation, the ghost just wanted the place to himself; in yet another, the ghost was in love with the current homeowner and he didn't want her to move (see chapter 7). In each case we were able to get the ghost to move on and the house sold within a week.

WHY AN EARTHBOUND GHOST MIGHT NOT WANT TO LEAVE

Here's what ghosts have taught me about what's keeping them stuck on this plane:

- They are afraid to face God because of some things they did in their life. They were taught that God is a punishing God, and they fear that they will be sent to hell for their bad behavior while living, so instead of going over and taking that chance, they stay here. They actually believe that God can't find them as long as they don't cross over!

- There is someone they do not like who has died, and they don't want to run into them in heaven. Many a ghost has told us that they don't want to run into their deceased ex-husband or ex-wife and that they would rather stay here.

- They think going to heaven is going to be a real drag. They think they will automatically become angels, and all the "fun in their life" will stop, so they decide to stay here and hang out with people who like to have a good time.

- They are afraid of letting go of their identity. They may have been someone important in their community, and they want to stay here and "hold on to their name."

- Some ghosts don't know they are dead! That's right. Some of them believe there is no such thing as life after death, so when their body dies and their soul comes out of the body, they don't know where to go. If an angel, spirit guide, or a deceased relative approaches them and tries to direct them over to heaven, they think they are hallucinating so they don't pay attention. They figure they couldn't possibly be dead because they feel so alive, and so they look around for a home to inhabit.

- They feel the strong pull of a loved one on this side, so they stay, thinking they are helping them in their grieving process.

- They stay to protect a loved one here.

- They don't want to leave a loved one.

- If they were murdered, they may stick around until justice has been served.

- If they died from addiction, they may hang around looking for a body to inhabit so they can continue their drug of choice.

How to Get Rid of a Ghost

Before I go into steps you can take to get rid of a ghost, I would like to share a newspaper article with you that one of my students gave me. Her great-aunt sent it to her back in the 60s. In some ways, we've come a long way in our understanding of ghosts, and in other ways, I think many people today still believe at least some of this ancient folklore:

In October 1965, the *Chicago Tribune* ran the following article on Halloween:

Sure-Fire Remedies to Rout an Uninvited Ghost

Halloween, traditionally the time for ghosties and ghouls and pesky things that go bump in the night, is just around the corner. Should you encounter any such phenomena and wish to be speedily delivered from them, we offer the following suggestions culled from ancient folklore. Sorry, but we can make no guarantees.

If bothered by a witch, throw salt on her, it burns like fire.

If a ghost crosses your path turn around three times and spit. Then address the specter in Latin. That will confuse the ghost and he or she will hurry out of the neighborhood.

Worried about ghostly visitation while you're asleep? Hang a flour sifter at the foot of your bed before nodding off. Any ghost wandering in will see the sifter and feel compelled to start counting the holes. By the time he's finished, it'll be dawn and the ghost will have to leave before he's had a chance to do any mischief.

Scatter black pepper around your bed; it keeps ghosts away. And last but not least, to repel ghosts—and probably anyone else for that matter—eat three garlic bulbs.

This article reminds me of a ghostbusting job Michael and I went on a few years ago. We got a call from some students in their early twenties who said they were part of the parapsychology department at one of our local colleges and that they had been called to investigate a haunted house in St. Paul.

The students had been told by some experts to pour flour all over the floor and that when the ghosts came in, they would leave flour prints wherever they went. They also hung pots and pans hanging from the ceilings, for the ghosts to make noise with, and a net, in hopes of catching one. None of these baits helped them to "catch" a ghost, however, and they wanted us to come and check it out.

The house did have ghosts, but they were all located upstairs. The ghosts weren't interested in walking through flour, playing with pots and pans, or being caught in a net. Remember, these are souls with some intelligence. They know what's going on. If they see flour all over the floor and leave flour prints, it's because they want to make a mess, not because they don't know any better.

As you've seen from these stories, I can actually see and hear spirits, but you do not need these abilities in order to rid your house of unwanted guests. In order to succeed at ghost cleansing, there are two things you should always remember:

- Your ghosts are unwelcome visitors in your home. Don't treat them like all-powerful beings from the world beyond who might get their feelings hurt if you confront them. They are not your friends or pets. They are stuck and need to move on.

- Being invisible does not make them powerful. They are not more powerful than you. But it is important not to look or act afraid when you confront your ghosts. Be firm when talking to them about leaving. Remember, they are souls, made of energy. You are the one with the body.

Step-by-Step Instructions for How to Get Rid Of a Ghost

1. Go to the room where you feel the spirit's presence the most strongly or where most of the activity occurs. If it doesn't frighten you, walk around the room and feel for a cold spot.

2. Tell the ghost that he needs to turn and go toward the white light. Tell him he is not welcome in your home and that you want him to leave. Tell him to look for angels who will assist him through the tunnel to the white light.

3. Ask for angels or deceased loving friends or relatives of this ghost to please come and assist him as he moves forward into the light. Wait for at least one or two minutes while friends and relatives gather around the ghost.

While you are waiting, tell the ghost that it is very important that he leave this plane of existence and get on with his life on the other side. As deceased friends and relatives gather, they will tell the ghost what to expect on the other side, thus calming the ghost's fears.

4. Often when this reunion takes place, the ghost becomes quite emotional, so you might want to lighten up your demands a bit. At this point in the ghostbusting, we usually become pretty gentle with the ghost and reassure him that he is making the right choice in leaving and going to the other side. Tell him you want him to follow his friends or relatives into the tunnel now. Tell him it is time to leave this place and get on with his life.

5. You might feel a slow, subtle difference in the room as the soul begins to let go and moves more and more into the light. Don't worry about whether or not you can feel it. It will be happening whether you sense it immediately or not. The ghost is leaving.

6. Open at least one window so that the sage and negative energy can exit. Next, take some sage or palo santo, not much more than a quarter of a cup, and put it loosely in either an abalone shell or in a clean ashtray. Light it in three or four places and blow out the fire. Continue

to blow on it. You want the smoke. Walk around the room blowing on the smoke, or use a feather, fanning the smoke gently out into the room. Don't blow too hard, though, because you don't want sparks flying or to set off the smoke detectors. You may want to disconnect the smoke detectors while saging the room and hook them back up when you're done.

7. While you are saging, ask God or the universe to please clear out all the negativity in the room. This will clear out the ghost's negative vibes and your negative vibes about the ghost.

8. For those of you wondering if you can use a smudge stick, yes, you can. A smudge stick often has two or three different herbs in it, such as lavender, fir, or cedar. Sage is known for taking the negativity out. Fir, cedar, and lavender are known for bringing good vibes or blessings into a room. We used smudge sticks when we first began, but my guides told us sage was quicker, and when you're doing a house that could have anywhere from one to ten to twenty ghosts, you want to do it quickly!

9. When you have saged the first room, you might want to go on and sage all the other rooms in your house. Often

when people have a ghost, they have a lot of fear, and those fear vibes can linger in a house just like the smell of cigarette smoke.

10. As a matter of fact, I recommend saging your house periodically just to keep it clear, especially after you've had an argument with someone or something traumatic has happened in the house. Sage will clear out the left-over vibes, so you won't think about the incident every time you walk into the room.

11. When you have finished clearing the entire house, ask God or the angels to please seal your house from top to bottom with a white protective light so that no more intruders will come into your home. This step is very important.

12. We have found that if you talk about your ghost a lot after getting rid of him, he sometimes thinks you want him back, and all of the activity starts over again. If you want to talk to someone about this experience, please talk about it away from your home or wherever the ghost was. Talk in terms of the ghost being gone; talk about him having safely made the passage and say that he is now happily on the other side. Do not sound as if you miss the ghost or wish he were still there.

13. Some people do miss the activity or excitement of having a ghost in their life, and they unwittingly ask them to come back. If you miss your ghost, please find something else to fill up that empty space in your life. Both you and the ghost need to get on with your separate lives.

CLEARING, PROTECTION, AND PRAYERS

Here are five suggestions to help you deal with everyday life, whether you have a ghost or not. The solution I recommend most often is the clearing exercise, so let's start there.

Clearing Exercise

One of the psychic gifts we are given is called clairsentience, or the gift of sensing. What that means is that a clairsentient can walk into a room and feel the vibes—he can feel what other people are going through and sense through his body what's going on with other people. A lot of people have this gift, and as a result they're walking around with others people's "stuff" all over them. The clearing exercise helps you get rid of this stuff. I think of it as a prayer or a request of the universe. It's a very simple exercise. All you do is take a relaxing breath in and release it. Then ask God or the universe, silently or out loud, to:

Please clear me

Please clear me

Take another calming breath in and out and ask:

Please clear my mind

Please clear my mind

Take another calming breath in and out and ask:

Please clear my body

Please clear my body

Take another calming breath in and out and ask:

Please clear my soul

Please clear my soul

Take another calming breath in and out and ask:

Please clear me psychically

Please clear me psychically

You can use this same basic exercise for clearing your home, your office, your car, your children, other loved ones, or whatever space feels or seems "off."

While it's very simple, it really works. You might think of it as a giant, invisible, energetic lint remover. You can do it as often as you want. If you are a particularly sensitive person, you might want to clear yourself whenever you've been around other people so that you don't carry their stuff around with you.

Mirror Necklace

If you are someone who picks up other people's energy, I strongly recommend that you wear a mirror necklace. The mirror faces outward and reflects any negative energy away from you. They are very inexpensive and well worth wearing. You can find them at the store on my website, *www.echobodine.com.*

Burning Sage or Palo Santo

This next solution involves burning the herb sage, which is a great "vibe cleanser," or palo santo, a holy wood from Peru. Some people believe that burning sage actually gets rid of ghosts, but it doesn't. It just gets the negative vibes out of the house—the anger, fear, or hostility from the ghosts or the people living in the house. The Native American Indians suggest opening a window or door so that the smoke and the negative vibes have some place to go. Whenever I clear a house of ghosts, I always follow up by walking through the entire house with sage smoke or palo santo. It makes the house feel squeaky clean on an energetic level!

I buy whole leaf Dalmatian sage that has been crushed, but there are many different kinds on the market. You can grow it in your garden, and in some places, you can pick it along the highway. Native American Indians suggest burning it in something made from the earth. I didn't know this for a long time and burned it in a pie pan. It was still just as effective. But now I use an abalone shell. Just take about a fourth of a cup of sage, put it in the shell (or other object), and light the sage. Once it catches on fire, gently blow it out. You actually want the smoke rather than the fire.

For those of you who haven't smelled sage before, I just want to warn you that it smells and looks like marijuana, which is why Michael and I switched to palo santo or Florida water. You can find these products at *www.moonwisdom.com*.

While holding the container, walk through your house, asking God or the universe to please clear it of any negative vibes or energy. I suggest that you use a feather to fan the smoke rather than directly blow on it, because you might blow too hard and have sparks flying all over, which is not safe. You also want to be mindful of smoke detectors.

The Squadron

If you suspect you have a ghost and would rather not try getting rid of them yourself, there is a very nice group of former ghosts who call themselves the Squadron. My spirit guides told me to call on them when I get a request for help from someone out of town. What you do is simply ask them out loud to please come to your home and get rid of the ghosts. They make house calls and their services are free. Over the years I've called on them many times and have always gotten very positive feedback from the homeowners.

I recommend that you call on the Squadron at night, because all of the activity in the home has calmed down, and they can come in and do their work when everyone's sleeping. Once they've come and gone (you can assume if you've asked for their help that they'll be there) ask for a healing angel to come in and fill up your house with white light of blessings and protection. Also ask them to seal the house up so that you won't be bothered by more intruders.

The biggest problem with this solution is that people don't believe the Squadron will really come to their house. They don't believe it's possible. Believe me, they have come every time I've called on them, and they know their stuff. It works.

Prayer for Protection

Finally, I think everyone should have a good prayer for protection. My psychic development teacher always used to say that if we ever felt scared by ghost or spirit activity, we should say a prayer that made us feel safe. Here's one I learned from the Unity Church, but of course you can use any prayer you like:

The Light of God surrounds me

The Love of God enfolds me

The Power of God protects me

The Presence of God watches over me

Wherever I am,

God is.

And all is well.

Demons and Evil Spirits

Some people are under the misconception that all ghosts are demonic or evil. *But only ghosts or spirits who were evil in their lives will be that way when they're dead.* We are in death the way we were in life, except that we are a little bit mellower and our perception changes when we die. Who we are here is basically who we are there.

In all my years as a ghostbuster, I have never met a demonic spirit. I have met some pretty negative, hateful spirits, but never one who I would call evil. Ghosts are souls. It is that simple.

One of my students asked me what evil spirits were, so I asked my guides for their definition. Here's what they had to say:

Unfortunately, there are many evil people on earth, people who have no regard for one another, perhaps who would love to see their fellow man fail, be hurt, or be tortured emotionally, mentally, or physically. People who hate clear through to their soul. People who have no conscience, no morals. No desire for good. The problem is that these people die and are souls who may or may not choose to go on to the other side.

They gave me a mental picture of a group of these evil spirits who all hang out together. Then they said, "They always hang out with their own kind, whether they're in the body or out." There is a universal law that says that like attracts like. Ghosts or spirits who hang around us will usually be similar to us. When we are living in the body, we hang out with other people who are similar to us in beliefs, morals, and values. That doesn't change in death.

As for green-eyed, frothy-mouthed, orange-slimed, demonic monsters, that'll cost you about twenty bucks for a movie ticket and popcorn. They only exist in the movies!

In Closing

We attract experiences that help our souls grow. If you have attracted ghosts to you, try to step back from the experience and look at it objectively. Look at how this experience might help you to grow in some area of your life. No experience is a waste of time. Look for the gem, the gift in the experience that might help you heal some issue, help enhance your self-worth, or help you feel more empowered.

This is what life is all about—creating situations to help us heal and grow. So pay attention and remember: You are more powerful than any ghost or spirit. You never have to be victimized by any of these earthbound souls, but the reality is always up to you.

I wish you nothing but the best on your journey.

—Echo Bodine

About the Author

Echo Bodine is a world-renowned psychic, spiritual healer, teacher, and ghostbuster. She is the author of *Hands that Heal, Echoes of the Soul, A Still Small Voice, The Key, The Gift, My Big Book of Healing,* and *Look for the Good and You'll Find God.* Bodine has been featured on NBC's *The Other Side, The Today Show, Sally Jesse Raphael, Sightings,* and *Encounters. Paranormal Borderline* did a feature on her family, calling them "the world's most psychic family."

For three years, Echo had her own radio show on FM107.1 in Minneapolis called *Intuitive Living.* She travels around the country teaching others how to recognize and develop their spiritual gifts.

She lives in Minnesota with her cat Susie.

Hampton Roads Publishing Company

. . . for the evolving human spirit

Hampton Roads Publishing Company
publishes books on a variety of subjects,
including spirituality, health, and
other related topics.

For a copy of our latest trade catalog,
call 978-465-0504 or visit our website at
www.hrpub.com